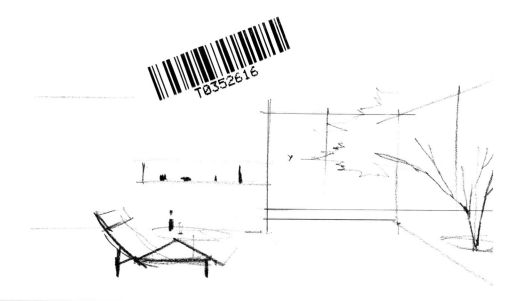

Interior Design
Presentations

Techniques for Quick, Professional Renderings of Interiors

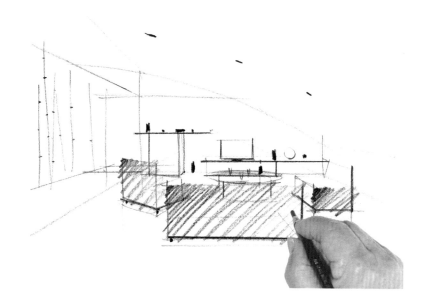

Preface

For those who are thinking about building a new house, it is the act of designing that house that becomes "the giant project". On the one hand those who build have a fixed vision, but on the other hand they are anxious and worried. Generally speaking, building a house is not an experience anyone goes through many times in a single lifetime. Hence, there are many unknowns. Under such circumstances it is crucial for an architect to make consultations with their clients "as easy as possible to understand".

Knowing all of this should make it clear that interior design sketches play a significant role in "visualizing" communications between you and your client. The ideal "visualizing" should take place during the initial consultation stage, especially when very little information is available. Your skill, or lack thereof, in sketching techniques is less significant here. What is important is that you actually manually render your client's dreams right before their eyes, regardless of your actual skill. In addition, we must note that if you neither draw nor use your interior design sketches, despite the fact that you are quite capable of actually creating relatively skilled sketches, then no one benefits. If interior design sketches are available, your client can agree or disagree with them right then and there. It helps immensely when a client can say "no" or "that is different from what I had in mind" during the initial consultation stage.

This is a how-to book on the means to effectively present architectural interior design ideas

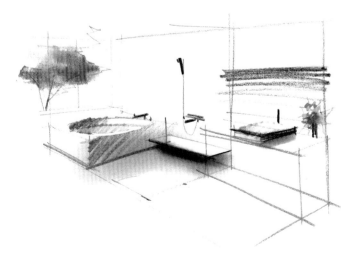

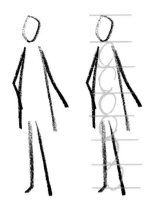

utilizing speedsketching. Rather than sketching fast by physically moving your hand very quickly, this book takes as its theme "how to simplify images for speedy rendering". This book introduces speedsketching by roughly dividing the total suggested time for a speedsketch into the following time segments: 10 sec., 1 min., 3 min., 5 min., 10 min. You must remember that the environment in which you will create your sketches is "public" and "in the presence of a client", which is to say that speedsketching is utilized as a means of communication.

Rather than drawing intently in silence, speedsketching is performed face-to-face while communicating with other people. Some people think that such short time periods as 10 seconds or 1 minute do not provide enough time to draw. However, I would say that time is a very interesting thing and since it is possible to have a simple conversation like "Good morning", "Fine weather today isn't it" in 10 seconds, then speedsketching for 10 seconds should be enough to draw a piece of furniture or a component.

In "1 whole minute", a complete lap of the second hand on a clock, I bet you can do more than you think. You can certainly communicate simple ideas or perhaps give someone the outline of a story you wish to tell. It is even enough time to take care of yourself. For example, you could cut your finger nails or clean your ears! In speedsketching, 1 minute is enough time to sketch a small room such as an entryway, a living room, a bedroom, a bathroom, or a powder room.

"3 minutes"—this is the amount of time that Ultraman (my favorite superhero from a TV series when I was young) can be active on earth. Younger generations (and foreign readers) might not be familiar with Ultraman, so I will give you another example. One round in a boxing match is 3 minutes long. That is a fairly long time, right? How each individual uses that time varies and can change depending on the nature of the task one is performing. However, it seems to me that most simple tasks can be completed in 3 minutes. In speedsketching, 3 minutes is enough time to draw multiple rooms, such as a living and dining room, living/dining and kitchen, dining and kitchen, etc.

One thing to be aware of is the fact that everything in our life has recently been sped-up (through computers, faster transportation, etc.), therefore "3 minutes" is not actually that short at all. The processing time of digital technology has decreased dramatically in recent years. Creating processing speeds that are fast beyond our wildest imagination is a wonderful thing and digital gadgets can now effortlessly draw sketches in the presence of a client. However, the issue here is that digital gadgets show only the end result, NOT the process. Manually sketching an interior design drawing on a piece of paper in front of a client can be seen as utterly inferior to what a digital gadget is capable of. However, the flexibility associated with manual rendering enables you to confirm, point-by-point, the multitude of desires your client might have. Also, in speedsketching, if you spend just a total of five minutes on a sketch you can even color it to closely resemble your client's wishes and present them with a quick glimpse of their dream.

Despite how technologically advanced our life is, the motions made by a human while drawing have not sped up that much. That being said, there is a great deal of comfort to be found in watching a person who is intently sketching in your presence. Careful though! Even if you really enjoy manual sketching, it will cause problems if you spend 30 minutes or an hour drawing while at a meeting with your client. So, let's always try to keep our drawings to about 10 minutes. In order to do this, you actually need to move your hand quite quickly. However, this requires quite considerable training. Therefore, the best thing to do is to figure out ways to simplify your lines and to "omit inessentials" in order to finish sketching quickly.

The really important thing when it comes to speedsketching is to change your viewpoint regarding sketching. Since sketching is done in front your client, as you communicate with them, obviously the sketching process is visible to your clients from beginning to end. So this type of sketch is never really "complete", rather it is "incomplete". The majority of architecture interior design drawings and perspective drawings place significance on how "complete" you draw (i.e. how many details you include). Contrary to this idea, speedsketches are fine with remaining "incomplete". They simply work as a sort of memo and serve as a means of communication. This book will explain the processes involved in creating these types of amazing interior design sketches.

You, as a designer, must remember to present your interior design advice WHILE carefully listening to your client's requests and preferences, and while taking their style of living into consideration. This book will help you in your endeavors by instructing you on methods for rendering not just household appliances, furniture, fixtures, lighting equipment, and small articles, but also people, pets, and plants. As our lifestyles continue to diversify into the future, I hope that you utilize speedsketching as your method of choice for conveying themes like "warmth", "calmness", and "living together with nature".

And remember, even though this book has labels to suggest the amount of time each sketch should take, more important than meeting such time limits is your ability to relax and communicate effectively with your client.

Table of Contents

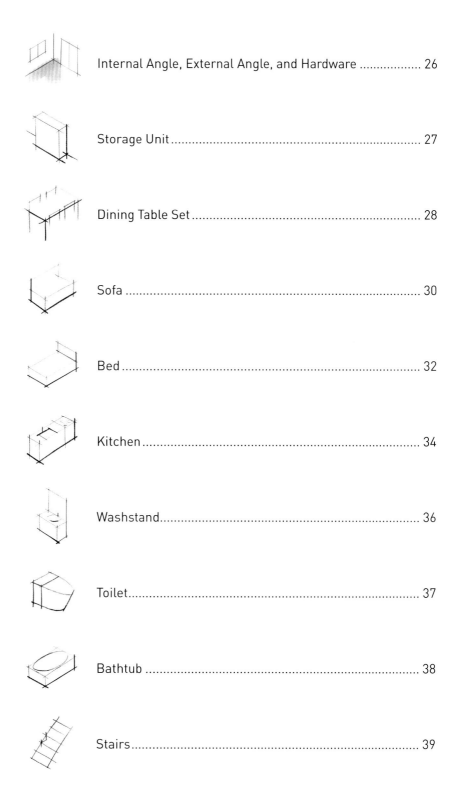

[1 Minute Sketch] Drawing an Interior Space

[3 to 5 Minute Sketch] Using One-point Perspective

Chapter 3 Key Points for Drawing

Chapter 4 Key Points for Coloring

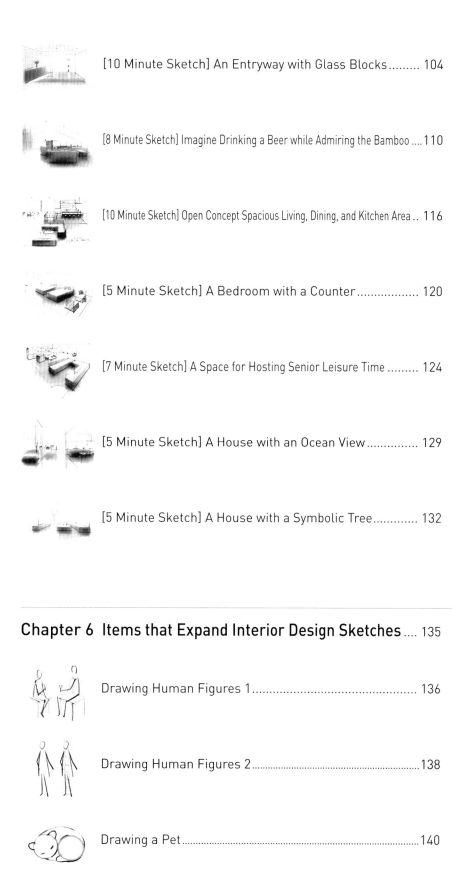

Chapter 6 Items that Expand Interior Design Sketches 135

Speedsketching Animation

 Let's Watch Some YouTube Videos
You can watch speedsketching videos.
Along this this book, please refer to the links below.

https://youtu.be/2seY110_Zj8
https://youtu.be/fE3LKXB4CQs
https://youtu.be/pU0yRgM2AqI

Chapter 1

Interior Design Sketch Gallery

This book elucidates speedsketching methods for architectural interior spaces. We begin with introducing images that "speedsketching could render".

Entryway and Exterior

[Entryway] Rendering the rise created by the piece of wood at the front edge of the entryway floor highlights the key sketching point of the entrance. Since there are many different elements incorporated into any entrance sketch—like doors, stairs, storage units, exterior landscapes, etc.—you need to simplify and organize everything in order to speed up the drawing process.

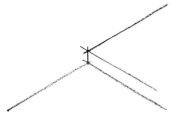

Entrance basics: Riser at the front edge of the entryway floor (10 sec.)

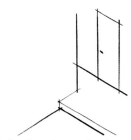

Placing the entryway riser in context with its surroundings (30 sec.)

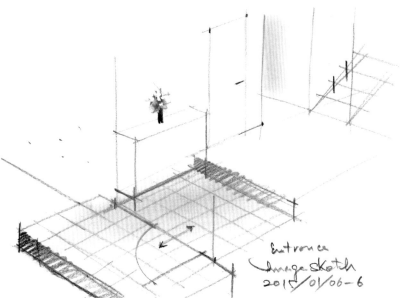

Rendering a scene so that the entrance is visible. Colored using pastels (see P. 72) (5 min.)

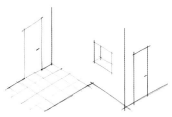

Use a peel-off color pencil (see P. 60) (1 min.)

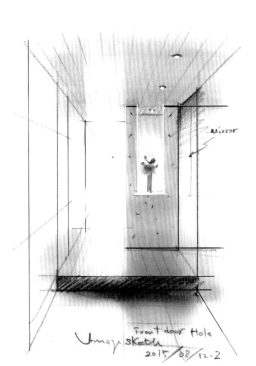

Pastels, color pencils (5 min.). A kneaded eraser is used to render light

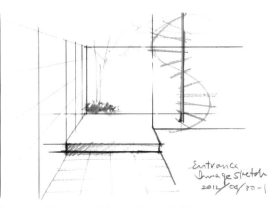

Entrance with a spiral staircase. Colored with pastels and color pencils (4 min.)

Pastels, color pencils (6 min.). A kneaded eraser is used to render light

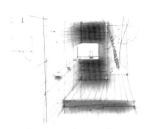

Pastels, color pencils (7 min.)

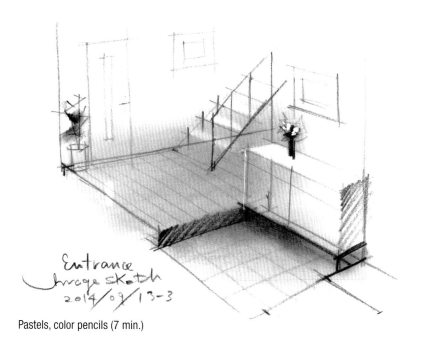

Pastels, color pencils (7 min.). A kneaded eraser is used to render light

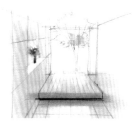

A see-through entrance that opens on a courtyard. Pastels (5 min.)

Pastels, color pencils (7 min.)

[Exterior] When sketching exteriors (exterior finishes, overall appearance), remember that they should complement the interior layout and that they should include outdoor plants to add character.

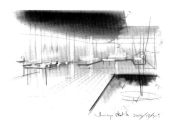

Patio dining area. Pastels (5 min.). Light was cast using a kneaded eraser

Pastels were used to sketch the sky and clouds (5 min.). The brightest areas were created using white-out

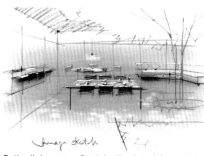

Patio dining area. Pastels (5 min.). A kneaded eraser was used to create sunlight filtering down through the trees

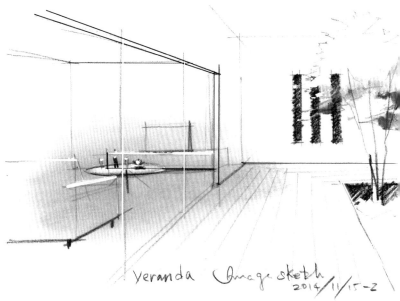

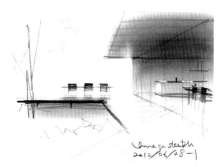

Outside dining area. Pastels. Draw plants simply (5 min.)

Veranda with a pleasant view of autumn leaves. Pastels (5 mins.). White-out was used to render the arms of the sofa

Living Room

This section includes items such as a sofa or storage units like TV stands. In addition, be sure to render light coming from any windows, and reflections on the floor. In order to create a sense of ease among your audience, the key is to draw using *contre-jour* (looking into the light). Generally, people prefer either the front or the side of a room to be bright.

Basic shape of a storage unit (10 sec.)

Basic outline of a sofa (10 sec.)

Bright and spacious, open concept, living room (10 min.)

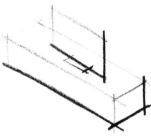

A TV stand (15 sec.)

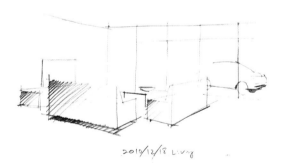

Pay attention to the strong and weak lines of the car (2 min.)

Layout with a grand piano. Simply sketched (5 min.)

While laying on a sofa, one might enjoy looking at cherry blossoms (5 min.)

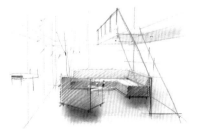

Open concept stairwell (7 min.)

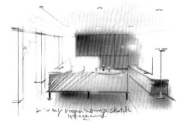

The storage unit was colored with pastels (7 min.)

Here we could enjoy looking at autumn leaves while sitting on the sofa (7 min.)

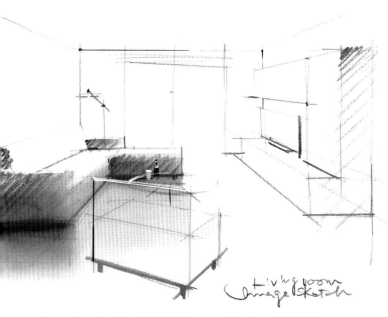

Be sure to make the chair in the foreground translucent (5 min.)

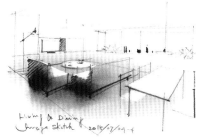

Colored with pastels to bring about a certain softness (7 min.)

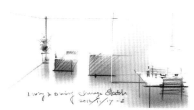

Use a kneaded eraser to strengthen the lighting of the dining area (8 min.)

Use pastels to emphasize the cherry blossoms (5 min.)

Use pastels to bring out softness and gentle warmth (5 min.)

Be sure to pay close attention to the reflection of the specially designed wall on the floor (7 min.)

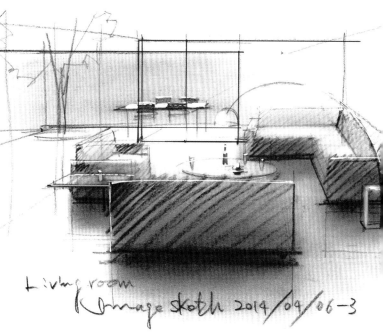

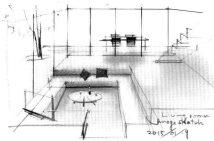

A spacious living room. Reduce the thickness of standard window frames by just using thin lines (10 min.)

For the outside patio table, feel free to use white-out to bring out the tabletop (10 min.)

Kitchen and Dining Area

Introducing kitchen and dining room layouts. Try to sketch while gauging the distance between the kitchen and dining area. Always try to simplify your kitchen counters and cabinets. The essential idea here is to quickly and clearly convey the overall image of the space.

The basic form of a kitchen counter (10 sec.)

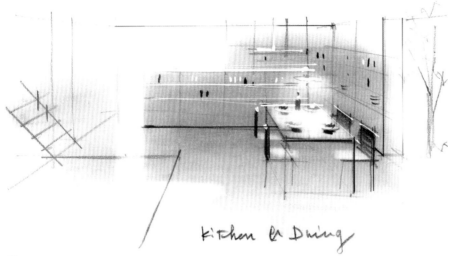

The kitchen sink is on the back side of the island, with storage facing us (7 min.)

The basic shape of a dining room set (20 sec.)

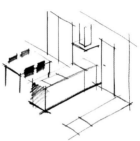

A memo-like sketch for a kitchen island and dining area (1 min.)

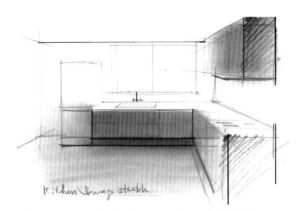

The kitchen cabinets were colored using pastels (4 min.)

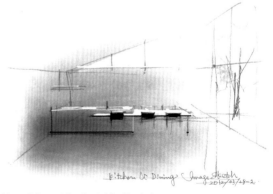

Use white-out for the table (5 min.)

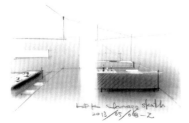

Split-level design. The dining area is on the lower floor (5 min.)

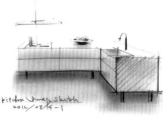

Colored with pastels (4 min.)

Create a sense of brightness using a kneaded eraser (5 min.)

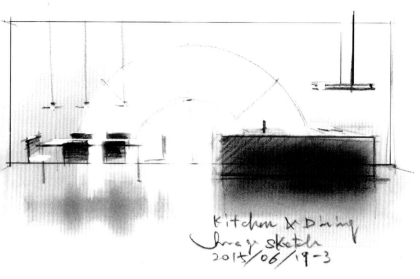

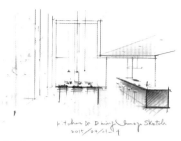

Spacious, open concept area (5 min.)

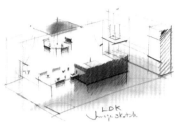

Use a kneaded eraser to render reflections from the windows on the floor (7 min.)

A dining and kitchen area with nostalgic windows (10 min.)

Sunny dining area (5 min.)

Drawing the staircase implies a certain flow toward the second floor (7 min.)

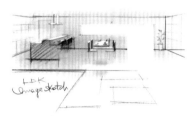

The key point here is the reflection of the window on the floor. Use a kneaded eraser (7 min.)

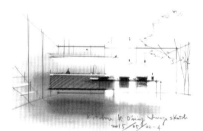

This scene was deliberately sketched from a low angle (7 min.)

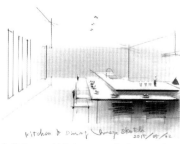

A dining and kitchen area that emanates a restaurant-like atmosphere (7 min.)

By purposefully making the right side dark, we can emphasize the brightness of the dining area (7 min.)

Living, Dining, and Kitchen Area

These areas combine to convey house usage, while allowing the homeowner's lifestyle to take center stage. Interior design sketches are crucial when attempting to share the sense of value the homeowner places on their living space, but also when allowing the homeowner and designer to come to a consensus on the overall design concept.

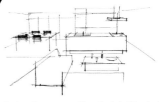

A simple, memo-like sketch (3 min.)

Color any key areas with color pencils (5 min.)

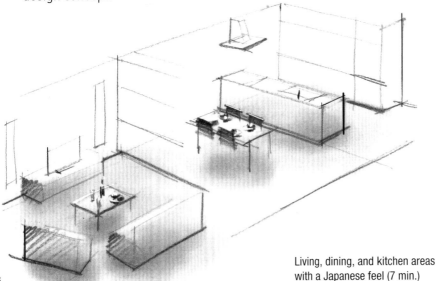

Use isometric drawing techniques to maintain precision (5 min.)

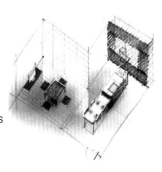

Living, dining, and kitchen areas with a Japanese feel (7 min.)

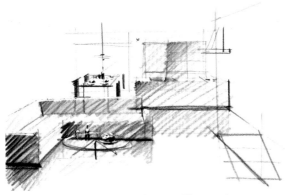

Bring about a manual rendering feel by adding rough coloring with color pencils (5 min.)

A house with a living room that has plenty play space (6 min.)

Color the sofa with a red colored pencil (7 min.)

This house has a built-in breakfast bar (10 min.)

Living, dining, and kitchen space where the furniture acts as a partition (10 min.)

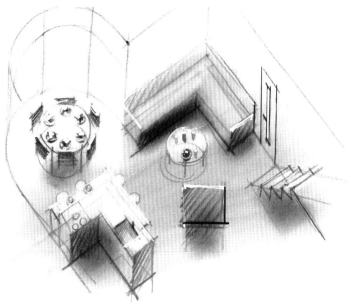

A house with a circular-shaped lounge (6 min.)

Here you can relax while enjoying autumn leaves (10 min.)

Open concept living, dining, and kitchen space (10 min.)

Spacious living, dining, and kitchen space (10 min.)

A house with tall windows (7 min.)

A spacious house with an ocean view (7 min.)

Here you can dine at a counter bar (7 min.)

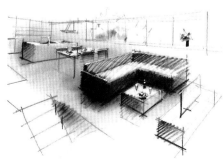

Long bay windows frame a second floor living, dining, and kitchen space (10 min.)

A great view with trees in the garden (10 min.)

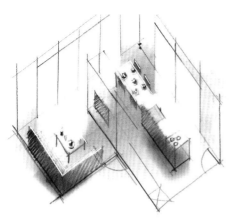

A space where the dining table and kitchen counter are placed next to each other (7 min.)

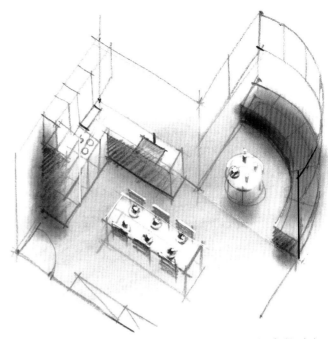

A house with an arced sofa (7 min.)

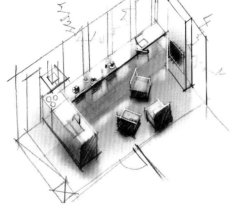

A space with a long counter (7 min.)

Teatime on a terrace (5 min.)

Colored living, dining, and kitchen space with an L-shaped kitchen counter (7 min.)

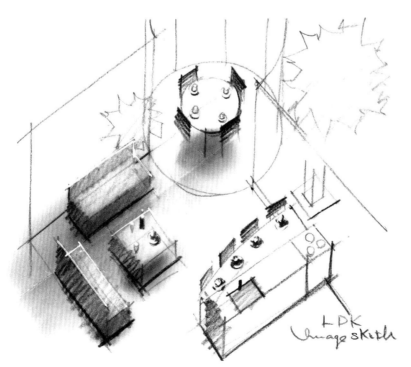

A house with a round breakfast bar (6 min.)

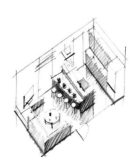

Here you can dine at a breakfast bar. The floor plan layout is quite compact (5 min.)

Bathroom

Bathrooms, lavatories, toilets—these spaces tend to be relatively small, so two or more are often combined. In this case, making the walls transparent strengthens the light ambiance of the room.

A basic toilet (10 sec.)

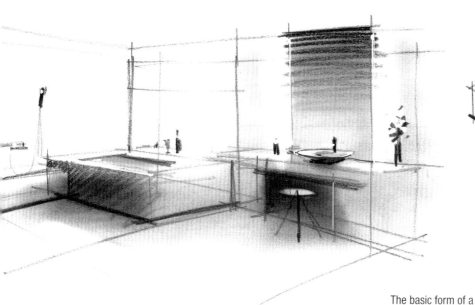

A simple bathtub (10 sec.)

The basic form of a washstand (10 sec.)

Use a kneaded eraser to create indirect lighting on the mirror (3 min.)

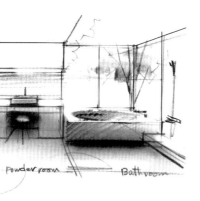

Use pastels to add color to the autumn leaves (5 min.)

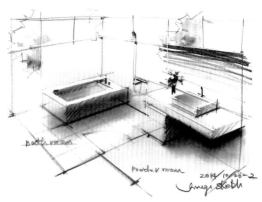

Render the autumn leaves using two pastels, yellow and red (7 min.)

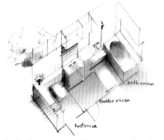

Including some nature in your bathroom adds to the overall ambience (7 min.)

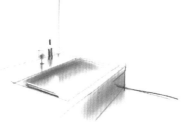

Relax and take a sip of wine (3 min.)

Use color pencils to add some vim and vigor (5 min.)

Bedroom

In order to convey to your clients how comfortable a bed is, be sure to draw it using different lineweights. By adding a sofa, bathroom, veranda, etc., your bedroom will come to look like a hotel suite.

A basic bed (10 sec.)

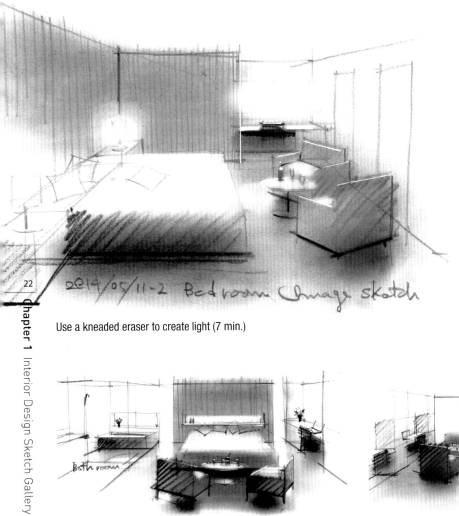

Use a kneaded eraser to create light (7 min.)

Omit any unnecessary lines (1 min.)

Draw using different lineweights (2 min.)

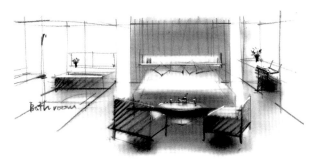

Draw the bedroom and bathroom together (10 min.)

A bedroom with a study (7 min.)

Use color pencils to add a touch of color to the beds (6 min.)

Here one can view autumn leaves as if they were on a "staycation" (7 min.)

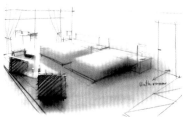

Use a kneaded eraser to bring out the softness of the beds (7 min.)

Chapter 2

Speedsketching Basics

In this chapter, we elucidate methods for sketching the fundamental elements that make up architectural interior design drawings.

While taking "how lines are simplified" as our theme, let's try to draw components, such as doors and windows, as well as furniture like sofas and tables, in our "[10 Second Sketch]" subsection. Additionally, we will introduce practical methods for drawing interior spaces by combining these elements in the subsections labeled "[1 Minute Sketch] Drawing an Interior Space", and "[3 to 5 Minute Sketch] Using One-point Perspective".

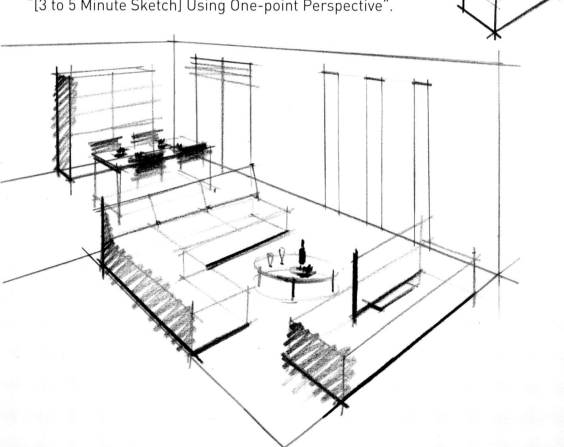

[10 Second Sketch]

Let's draw furniture, components, and appliances in about 10 seconds just by simplifying our lines. Rather than just quickly throwing down a bunch of lines to create your drawings, we believe that using the minimum number of lines necessary is crucial. At a consultation, simplified interior design sketches can be very effective because you can draw while still communicating effectively with your client. For the most part, perpendicular and angled (30 degree) lines make up the interior design sketch. With these lines it is important to be decisive and draw boldly without worrying about leaving some portions jutting out.

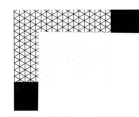

Make a photocopy of P.152 and lay it under your paper. Doing so will help you learn how to better draw angled lines.

Twelve Basic Sketches

Aside from the items introduced here, we should note that there is a huge variety of appliances, furniture, hardware, etc. Using the 10 second mark as an indicator, let's try to master techniques and approaches for simplifying images. You can then expand on these techniques and apply them to items not covered in this section.

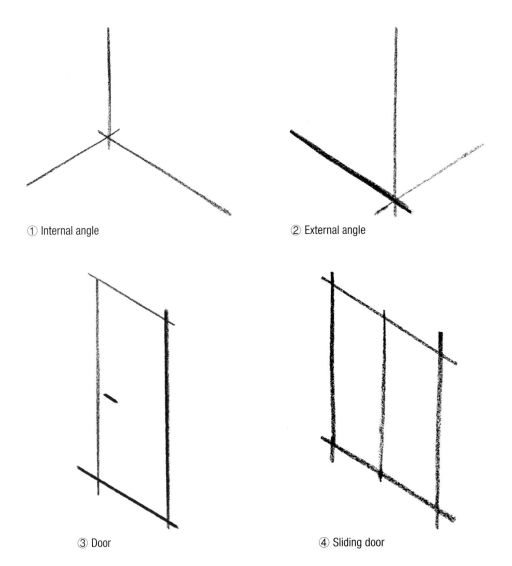

① Internal angle

② External angle

③ Door

④ Sliding door

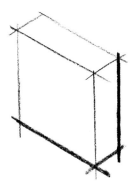

⑤ Storage unit

⑥ Dining table set

⑦ Sofa

⑧ Bed

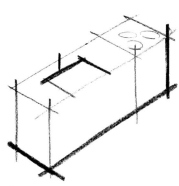

⑨ Kitchen

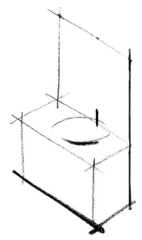

⑩ Washstand and mirror

⑪ Toilet

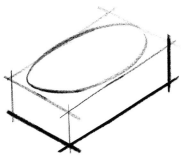

⑫ Bathtub

Internal Angle, External Angle, and Hardware

The simple composition involved in a basic living space.

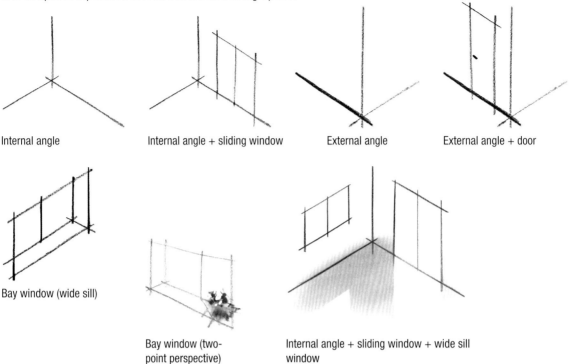

Internal angle   Internal angle + sliding window   External angle   External angle + door

Bay window (wide sill)

Bay window (two-point perspective)

Internal angle + sliding window + wide sill window

How-to draw a door

① Draw a perpendicular line and a line that slopes downward to the right

② Draw a perpendicular line on the right

③ Draw a bottom line that also slopes downward to the right

④ Draw a short line for the door handle to finish

How-to draw a sliding window

① Draw a perpendicular line and a line that slopes downward to the right

② Draw another perpendicular line

③ Draw a bottom line that slopes downward to the right

④ Draw a perpendicular line at the center to finish

How-to draw a wide sill window

① Draw a perpendicular line and a slightly long line downward to the right

② Draw a perpendicular line on the right

③ Draw a bottom line downward to the right

④ Draw a perpendicular line down the center to finish

This is one of the most basic pieces of furniture. By changing the length, height, and depth of a storage unit, you can in turn greatly change its shape and function.

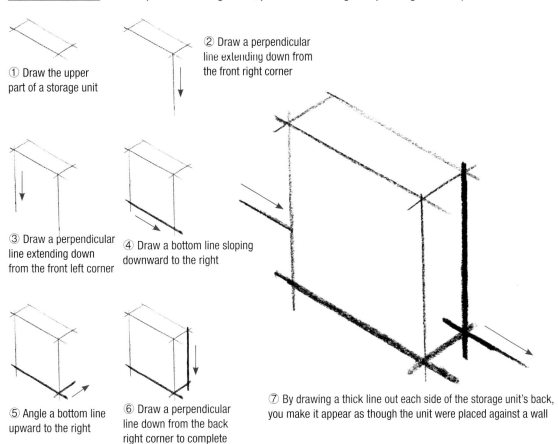

① Draw the upper part of a storage unit

② Draw a perpendicular line extending down from the front right corner

③ Draw a perpendicular line extending down from the front left corner

④ Draw a bottom line sloping downward to the right

⑤ Angle a bottom line upward to the right

⑥ Draw a perpendicular line down from the back right corner to complete

⑦ By drawing a thick line out each side of the storage unit's back, you make it appear as though the unit were placed against a wall

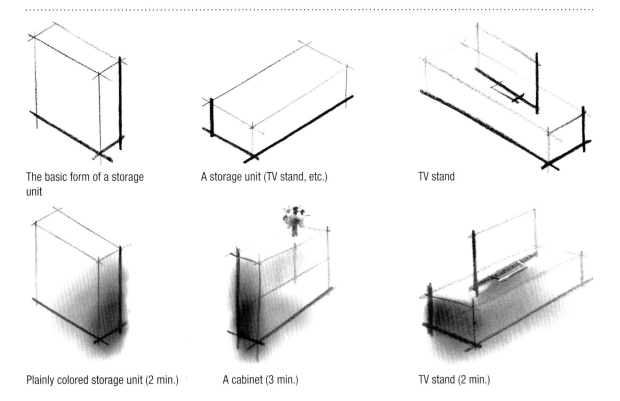

The basic form of a storage unit

A storage unit (TV stand, etc.)

TV stand

Plainly colored storage unit (2 min.)

A cabinet (3 min.)

TV stand (2 min.)

Dining Table Set

The key to quickly drawing a dining table set is knowing how to simplify the chairs. Just sketch the back of each chair! Omit the seat and legs.

Color the chairs with color pencils (4 min.)

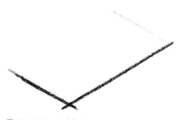

① Sketch a tabletop

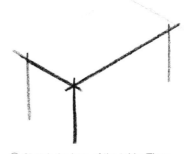

② Sketch the legs of the table (Three legs is fine)

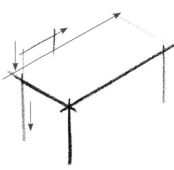

③ Sketch a chair. Make the back of the chair parallel to the tabletop and legs

④ While paying attention to overall balance, add second chair

⑤ Sketch two chairs in the foreground. Omit the seats

⑥ Our dining set is complete

Colored with pastels (5 min.)

An example of a round table

A round table and chairs

Let's practice sketching chairs by changing their direction

Pastel colored chair examples

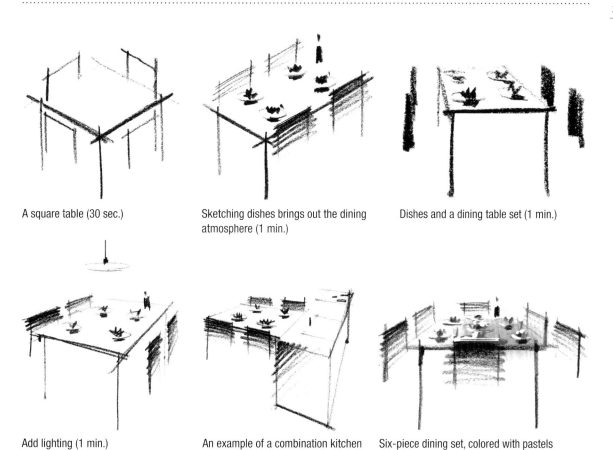

A square table (30 sec.)

Sketching dishes brings out the dining atmosphere (1 min.)

Dishes and a dining table set (1 min.)

Add lighting (1 min.)

An example of a combination kitchen counter and dining table (2 min.)

Six-piece dining set, colored with pastels (3 min.)

When we draw a sofa, we cannot help but unintentionally become sticklers regarding the design and comfort of the sofa. That is why we tend to draw excessive details. However, when we are trying to finish sketching in 10 seconds, we need to omit unnecessary lines and render everything quickly and simply. You can leave the finer characteristics and detailed image of the sofa's design until your next meeting with the client.

① Draw the seat of a sofa

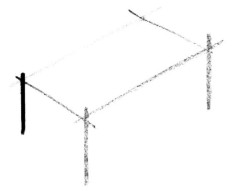

② Add thickness to the sofa

③ Draw lines for the bottom

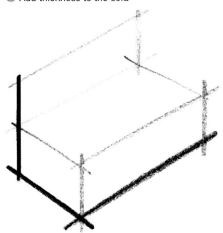

④ Draw the back to complete

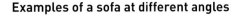

Examples of a sofa at different angles

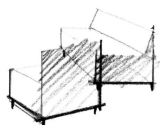

L-shaped sectional sofa (1 min.)

Colored with pastels (3 min.)

Colored with pastels + color pencils (4 min.)

Colored with pastels + color pencils (4 min.)

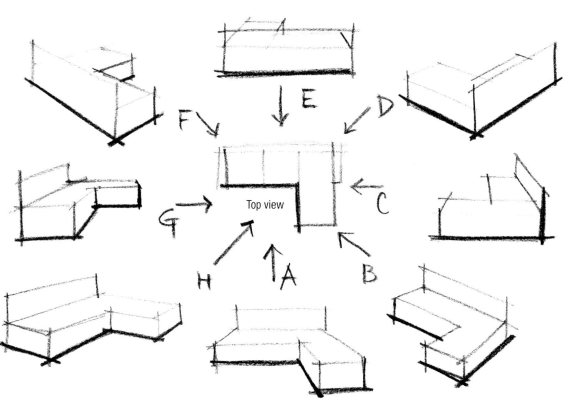

Variations from eight different angles

Similar simplifications to those introduced on the previous page are used to simplify our bed. The back of the sofa becomes the headboard for the bed.

① Draw the top of the mattress

② Draw downward lines perpendicular

③ Be sure to remain cognizant of the mattress thickness

④ Draw a line upward towards the right

⑤ Include the base of the headboard

⑥ The top of the headboard mimics the base

⑦ To complete, draw the downward sloping right post in one go

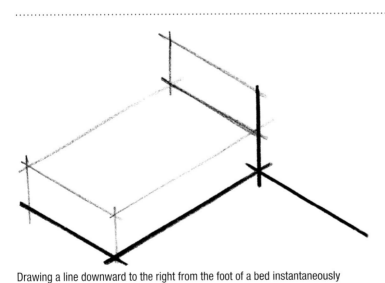

Drawing a line downward to the right from the foot of a bed instantaneously finishes the sketch of our bedroom (additional 1 sec.)

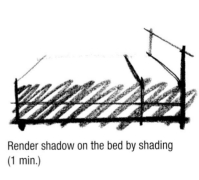

Render shadow on the bed by shading (1 min.)

Example: The thickness of the mattress is omitted

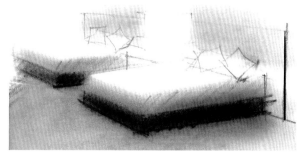

By coloring with pastels, the atmosphere of the bedroom is brought out (5 min.)

Use a kneaded eraser to add light to the top of each bed (5 min.)

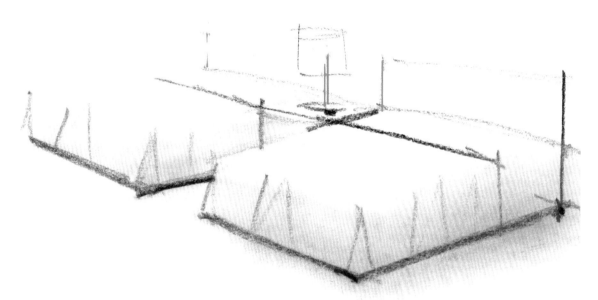

Soft and fluffy beds drawn in two-point perspective

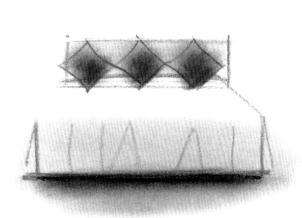

Add shams and don't be afraid to get fancy (3 min.)

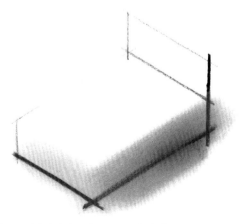

Use pastels to bring about a certain fluffy feel (1 min.)

Kitchen Omit cabinets, range hoods, backsplashes, and door layouts. Just draw the minimal number of elements to show that your sketch is obviously a kitchen. If necessary, replace omitted elements at the next meeting with your client.

① Draw a countertop

② Draw three downward lines perpendicular to the countertop

③ Draw two lines to represent the width and length

④ Draw a simple kitchen sink and faucet

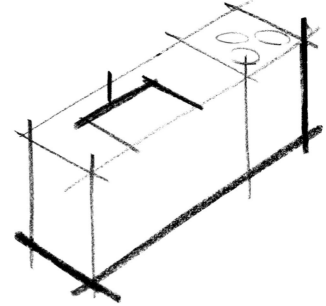

⑤ Draw a kitchen stove

⑥ To complete, add a stove top that extends horizontally (10 to 15 sec.)

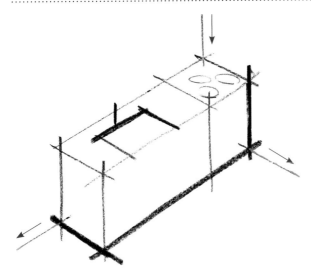

Here, we draw three lines so that it appears as though the kitchen counter is in the corner of the room

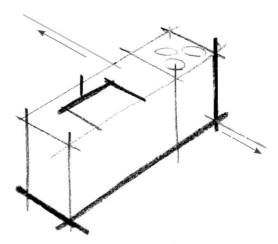

Here, we draw two lines so that it looks like the counter is an island

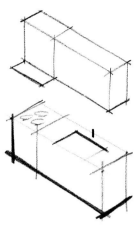

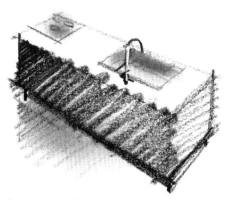

Add cabinets and a range hood

Example: A kitchen island combined with a simple ceiling mounted range hood (20 sec.)

Drawn in two-point perspective, colored with pastels and color pencils (2 min.)

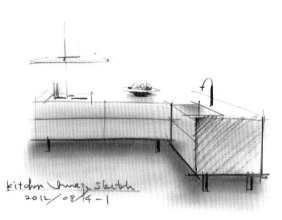

Drawn in two-point perspective, colored with pastels (3 min.)

Drawn in one-point perspective, colored with pastels (4 min.)

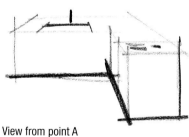

View from point A

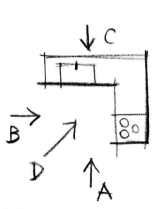

L-shaped kitchen: top view

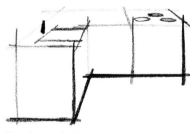

View from point B

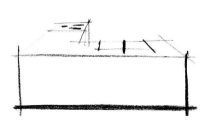

View from point C

View from point D

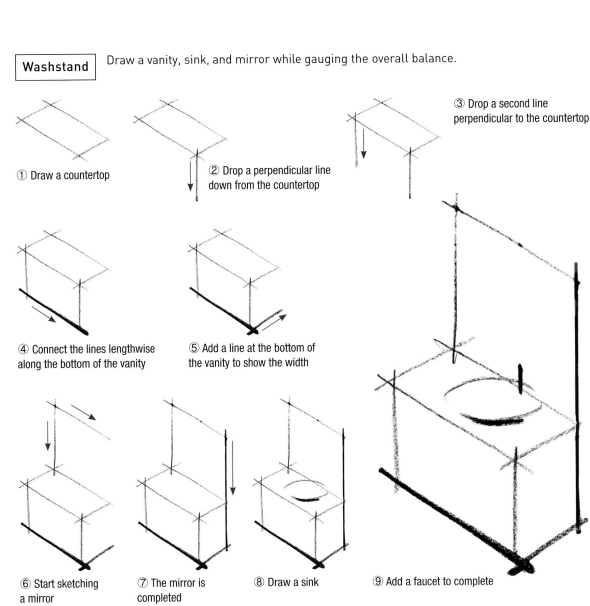

① Draw a countertop

② Drop a perpendicular line down from the countertop

③ Drop a second line perpendicular to the countertop

④ Connect the lines lengthwise along the bottom of the vanity

⑤ Add a line at the bottom of the vanity to show the width

⑥ Start sketching a mirror

⑦ The mirror is completed

⑧ Draw a sink

⑨ Add a faucet to complete

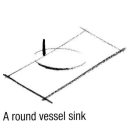

A round vessel sink

A square vessel sink

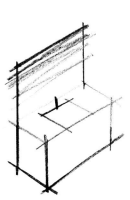

Create a mirror by shading

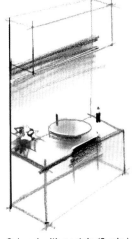

Colored with pastels (3 min.)

Colored with pastels (3 min.)

Toilet The key point when rendering the toilet bowl is to draw the curve as smoothly and well-balanced as possible.

① Draw the top section

② Fix the height of the toilet based on the width of the top you drew

③ Draw another line

④ Draw width

⑤ Draw a "mirror symmetry" curve to create the top of the bowl

⑥ Draw a line angled down and inward

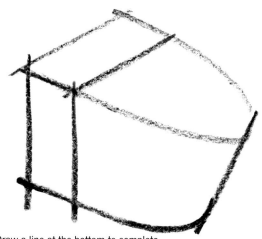

⑦ Draw a line at the bottom to complete

The most simplified sketch possible

Vary the lineweight to create a more expressive object

Simplified sketch of a tank and a toilet bowl

Simplified sketch of tank-less toilet bowl

Tank-less toilet bowl. Colored with pastels (2 min.)

Add emphasis to the lines. Colored with pastels (1 min.)

Add more emphasis to the lines. Colored with pastels (1 min.)

A toilet bowl with a tank. Colored with pastels (1 min.)

Tank-less type. Colored with pastels (2 min.)

Bathtub | Though bathtubs come in many different designs, you will often find yourself drawing a simple oval-shaped tub, as in this section. It is important to draw the oval as big as possible, as if it were protruding from its casing.

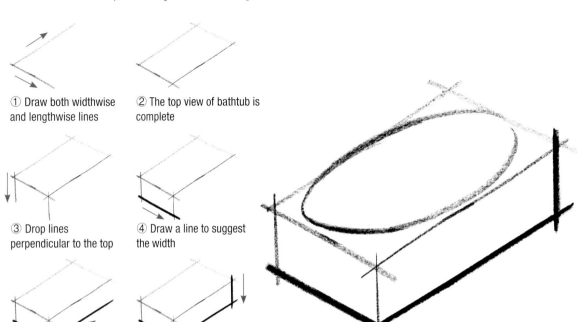

① Draw both widthwise and lengthwise lines

② The top view of bathtub is complete

③ Drop lines perpendicular to the top

④ Draw a line to suggest the width

⑤ Draw a line to suggest the length

⑥ Drop a final line down, perpendicular to the top

⑦ Draw a large oval to complete

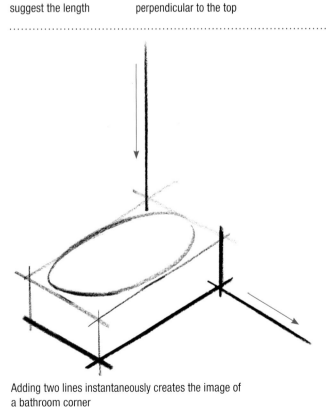

Adding two lines instantaneously creates the image of a bathroom corner

END

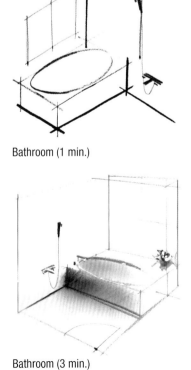

Bathroom (1 min.)

Bathroom (3 min.)

Stairs	Besides the twelve basic items introduced up to this point, stairs are definitely another item that we need to know how to draw. The key point to stairs is simplifying the risers and treads.

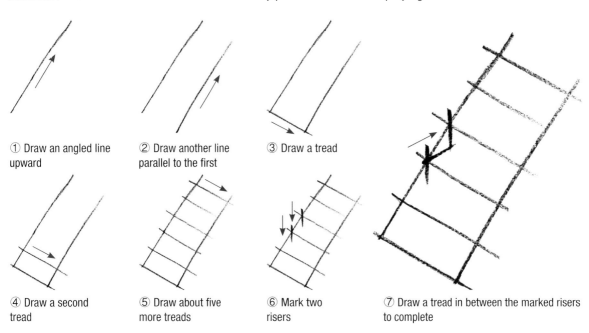

① Draw an angled line upward

② Draw another line parallel to the first

③ Draw a tread

④ Draw a second tread

⑤ Draw about five more treads

⑥ Mark two risers

⑦ Draw a tread in between the marked risers to complete

A wall and stairs: A

A wall and stairs: B

Colored with pastels (2 min.)

Landing A

Landing B

Landing C

① [1 Minute Sketch] Drawing an Interior Space

Let's try to finish drawing an interior space in just 1 minute. This method is a combination of 10 second Speedsketch basics. Since this is just a sketch used as a simple means of communication during an initial consultation, it will serve its purpose as long as key elements are sketched out. It is unnecessary to include each and every element found in our interior space.

| Entryway | The key point of any entryway is to render the gap that the riser creates at the front edge of entrance. |

① Draw a storage unit

② Add the riser

③ By drawing a perpendicular line, we complete the left wall

④ Render a hallway with single lengthwise line

⑤ Draw a door

⑥ Cast shadows (with shading) on the storage unit to complete (1 min.)

Colored with pastels (5 min.)

① Draw a cuboid

② Add the riser

③ Add the top of the stair

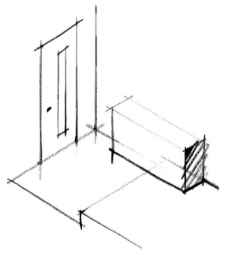

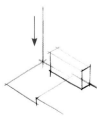

④ Draw a single line to create the left wall

⑤ Add a front door

⑥ Cast shadows (with shading) on the storage unit to complete (1 min.)

① Draw a storage unit

② Draw an internal angle and a TV

③ Draw sliding doors

④ Add a sofa

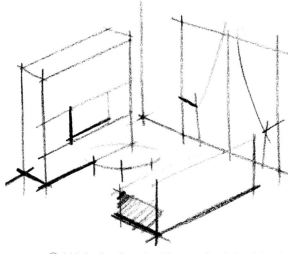

⑤ Add a table

⑥ Draw curtains to complete

⑦ Add shading throughout the completed sketch (1 min.)

41

① Draw a TV stand

② Draw a line for the wall

③ Draw a three-seater sofa

④ Draw a chair

⑤ Draw a coffee table to complete

⑥ Add shading to the completed sketch (1 min.)

Colored with pastels and color pencils (4 min.)

Kitchen and Dining Room

Cooking and eating are related daily activities. In order to clearly illustrate the relationship between these activities, we need to practice drawing kitchen counters and dining tables together.

① Draw a kitchen counter

② Draw a range hood

③ Draw two floor lines to make a kitchen island

④ Draw a dining table

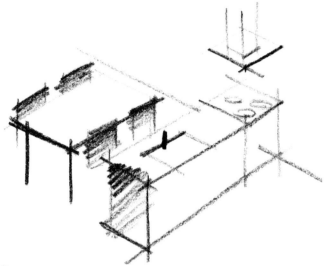

⑤ Draw chairs to complete (approx. 1 min.)

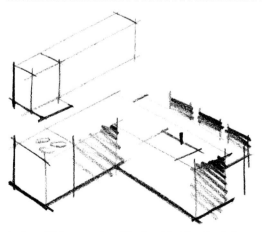

L-shape kitchen counter with a breakfast bar (1 min.)

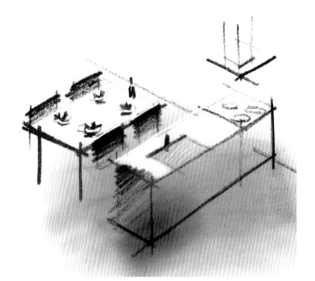

Draw dishes and color with pastels and color pencils (approx. 3 min.)

① Draw a kitchen counter

② Draw two lines to sketch out the wall that is next to the kitchen counter

③ The ceiling height is approximately three times the kitchen counter height

④ Draw a kitchen cabinet

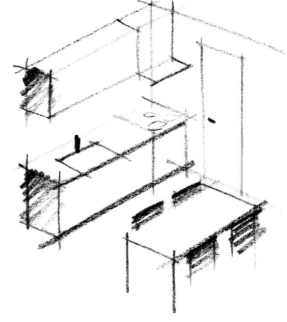

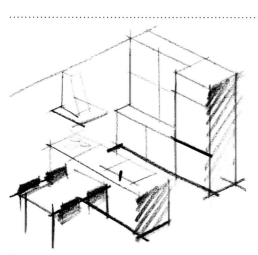

⑤ Add a dining set

⑥ Add a door to complete (approx. 2 min.)

Downward view from the dining set side (2 min.)

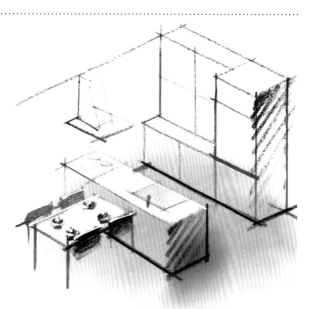

Draw dishes, and color with pastels + color pencils (total approx. 3 min.)

Bedroom For a bedroom, the balance between the bed and the bedroom furniture is crucial. We need to constantly consider the various sizes of the furniture that we want in our bedroom.

① Draw a bed

② Draw a nightstand

③ Draw a bedside lamp

④ Draw another bed

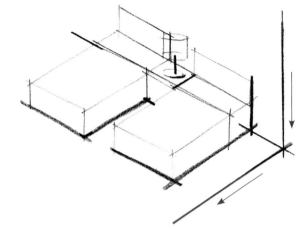

⑤ Draw a floor line to make your bedroom

⑥ Draw wall lines to complete (1 min.)

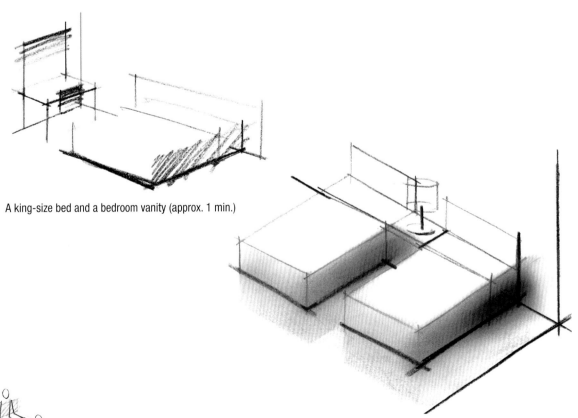

A king-size bed and a bedroom vanity (approx. 1 min.)

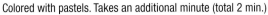

Colored with pastels. Takes an additional minute (total 2 min.)

It is obvious that we need to include a bathtub in a bathroom, but we also need to include a multifunctional faucet and a shower head in simplified form. Additionally, let's challenge ourselves by trying to add a potted plant by the window.

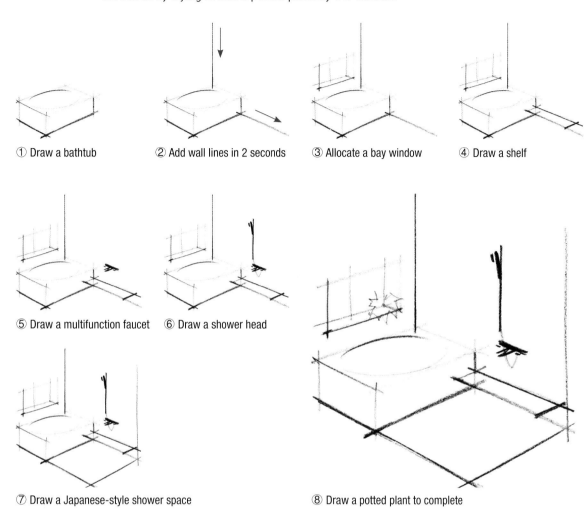

① Draw a bathtub

② Add wall lines in 2 seconds

③ Allocate a bay window

④ Draw a shelf

⑤ Draw a multifunction faucet

⑥ Draw a shower head

⑦ Draw a Japanese-style shower space

⑧ Draw a potted plant to complete

Simplified form of a shower head

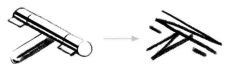

Simplified form of a multifunctional faucet

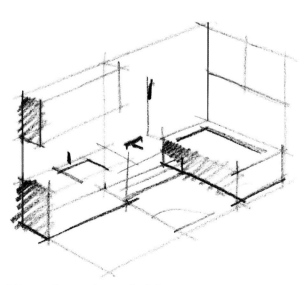

Add a powder room (approx. 2 min.)

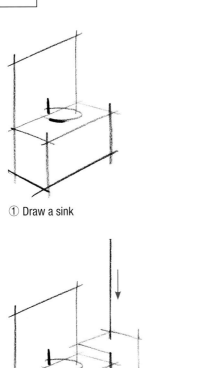

① Draw a sink

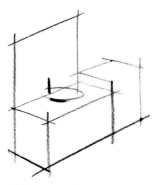

② Draw a washer

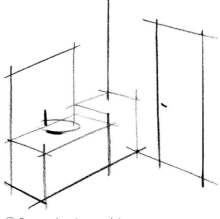

③ Draw a wall

④ Draw a door to complete

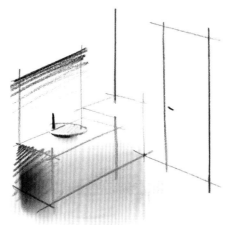

Colored with pastels + color pencils. Takes an additional minute (total 2 min.)

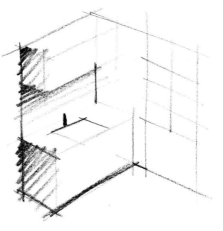

On the right is a wall storage unit (1 min.)

Bathroom Practice drawing a toilet and a washstand in the same room.

① Draw a toilet (tank-less type)

② Draw a floor line

③ Draw a storage unit

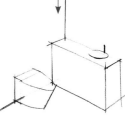

④ Draw a wall line and a sink

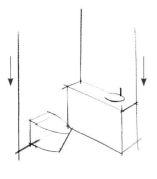

⑤ Draw two wall lines

⑥ Draw two ceiling lines

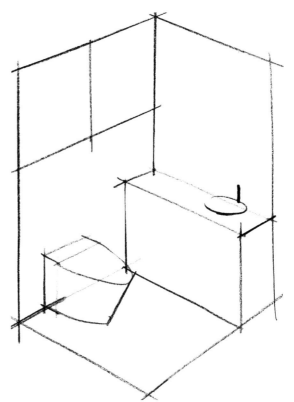

⑦ Draw a window to complete

47

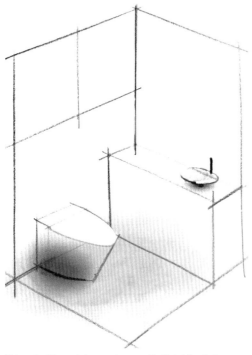

Colored with pastels + color pencils (total 2 min.)

⏱ [3 to 5 Minute Sketch] Using One-point Perspective

Make a photocopy of the one-point perspective template on P.155 and lay it under some paper to help you to gauge perspective balance.

| Livingroom | This is a living room of approximately 157 ft^2. The composition is very simple, with just a sofa, a TV stand, and a coffee table. Feel free to add curtains, lights, indoor plants, etc. The material used in this section is oil-based peel-off pencil (Mitsubishi Dermatograph No. 7600). |

Sample Layout

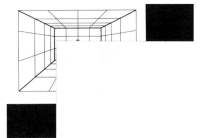

① Place A4 (letter) size blank paper on the copied template

② Draw a forward facing wall

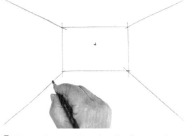

③ Trace the template for the floor and wall lines

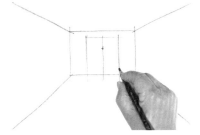

④ Draw a sliding door

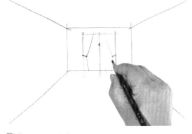

⑤ Draw curtains

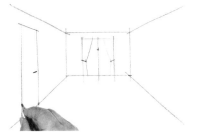

⑥ Draw a door

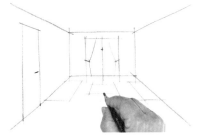

⑦ Layout the furniture

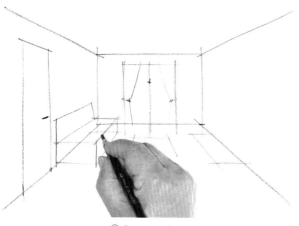

⑧ Draw a sofa

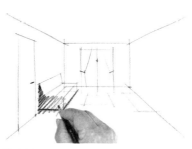

⑨ Add sharpness to the sofa and create some nuanced shading

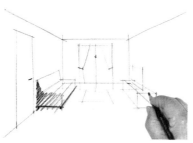

⑩ Draw a TV stand

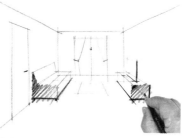

⑪ Add sharpness to the TV stand and add shading

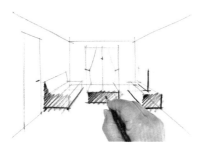

⑫ Draw a coffee table

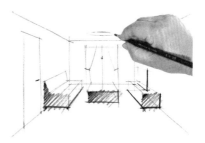

⑬ Draw a light fixture on the ceiling

⑭ Draw light stands, indoor plants, dishes, etc., to complete

③ Execution time: Approximately 3 minutes

Dining and Kitchen Space

This dining and kitchen space is approximately 196 ft². The composition consists of a kitchen counter, a dining table set, a fridge, and a china cabinet. If you have extra time, feel free to add lights, kitchen appliances, dishes, etc.

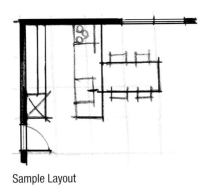

Sample Layout

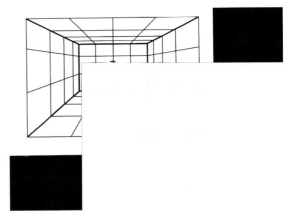

① Place an A4 (letter) sized piece of blank paper on a copied one-point perspective template (P.155)

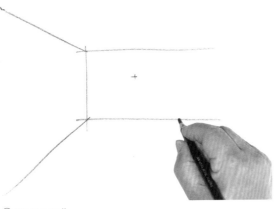

② Draw a wall

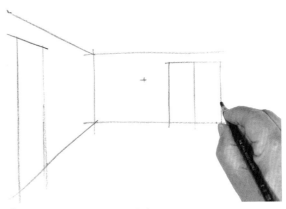

③ Draw a door and sliding window

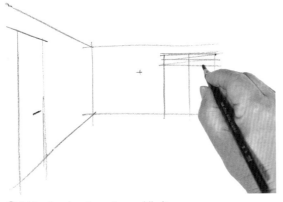

④ Add a door handle and some blinds

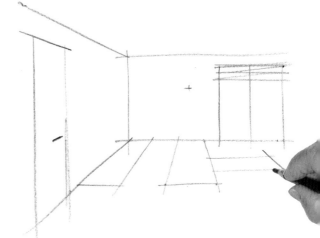

⑤ Layout the furniture and appliances

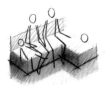

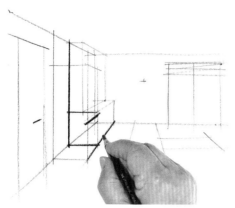

⑥ Draw a china cabinet

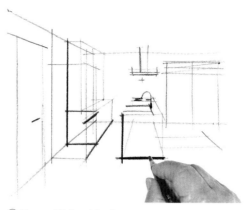

⑦ Draw a kitchen island

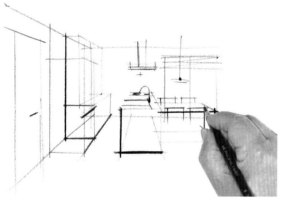

⑧ Draw a dining table set

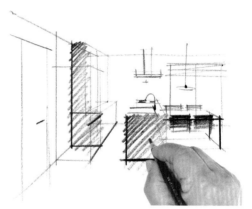

⑨ Add graduated shadows to complete

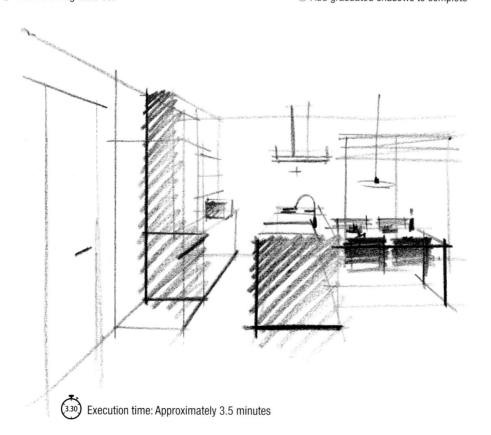

(3.30) Execution time: Approximately 3.5 minutes

⏱ (3·5) [3 to 5 Minute Sketch] Using Isometric Projection

Living, Dining, and Kitchen Space

This living, dining, and kitchen space is approximately 314 ft². It is intended for senior living. If you have extra time, feel free to add lighting, kitchen appliances, and dishes. Make a photocopy of the isometric projection template on P.155 and lay it under blank paper to help you gauge perspective balance.

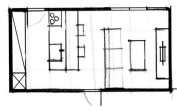

Sample Layout

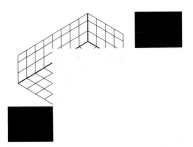

① On the copied template, place A4 (letter) sized blank paper

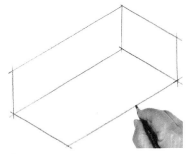

② Trace the guide for the lines that compose the walls and floor

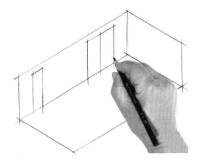

③ Add a door and sliding window

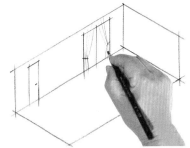

④ Add a door handle and curtains

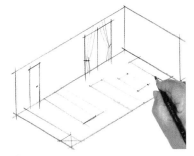

⑤ Layout furniture and appliances

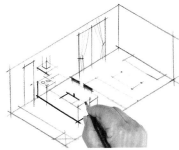

⑥ Draw a kitchen counter and breakfast bar

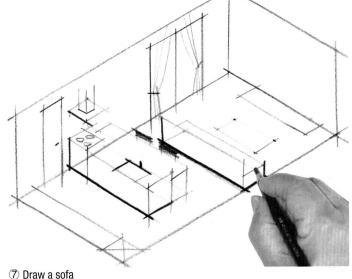

⑦ Draw a sofa

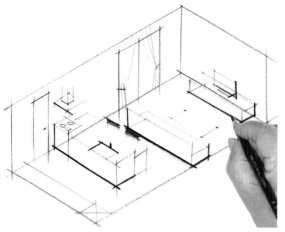

⑧ Draw a TV stand

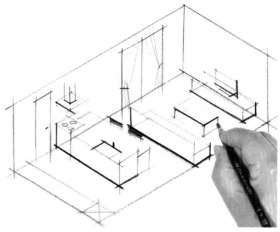

⑨ Draw a coffee table

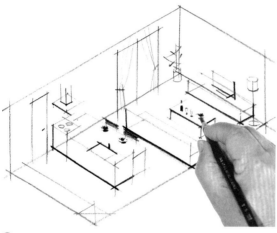

⑩ Draw light stands, indoor plants, dishes, etc.

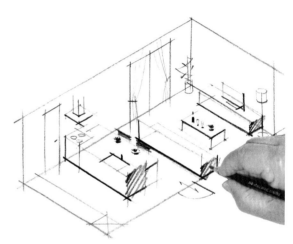

⑪ Cast shadows by adding some shading to complete

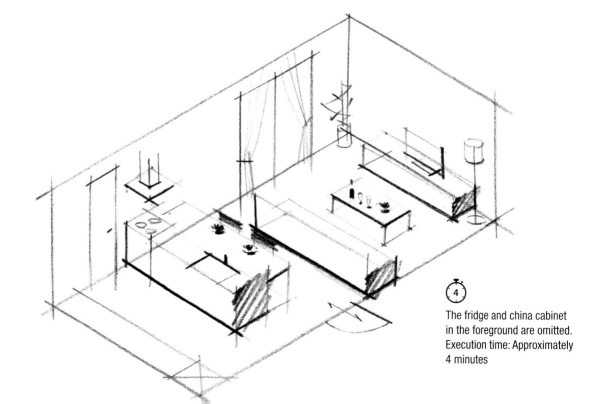

The fridge and china cabinet in the foreground are omitted.
Execution time: Approximately 4 minutes

⏱ [3 to 5 Minute Sketch]
Using Two-point Perspective

Dining and Kitchen Space

This dining and kitchen space is approximately 196 ft². The composition consists of a kitchen counter, a dining table set, a fridge, and a china cabinet. If you have extra time, feel free to add lights, kitchen appliances, dishes, etc. Make a photocopy of the two-point perspective template (157 ft²) on P.156 and lay it under blank paper to help you gauge perspective balance.

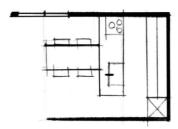

Sample Layout

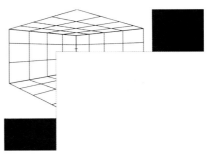

① Place A4 (letter) sized blank paper on the copied template

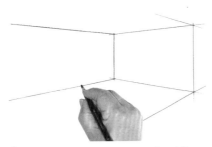

② Trace the guide lines for the wall and floor

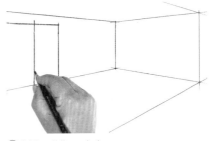

③ Add a sliding window

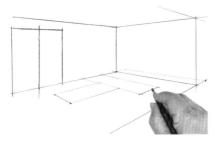

④ Layout a kitchen counter and dining table

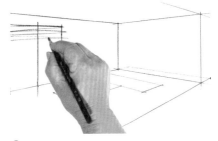

⑤ Draw some blinds

⑥ Draw a fridge, a china cabinet

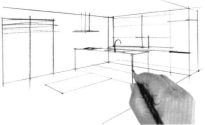

⑦ Draw a kitchen counter

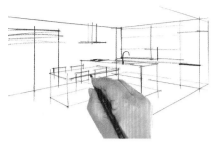

⑧ Draw a dining set

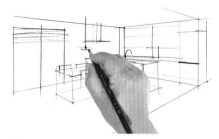

⑨ Draw some lighting

⑩ Fill in the back of the chairs by shading

⑪ Add plates, appliances, dishes, etc.

⑫ Cast shadows on the kitchen counter and the fridge

⑬ Erase unnecessary lines with white-out to complete

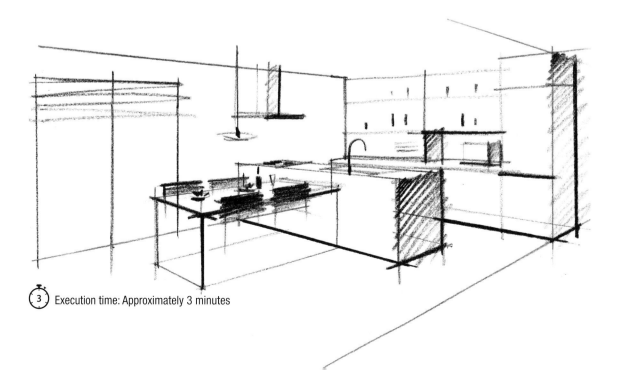

③ Execution time: Approximately 3 minutes

Make a photocopy of the two-point perspective template (314 ft²) on P.157 and lay it under some blank paper to help you gauge perspective balance.

Sample Layout

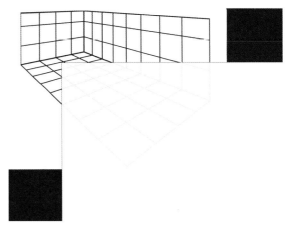

① Place A4 (letter) sized blank paper on the copied template

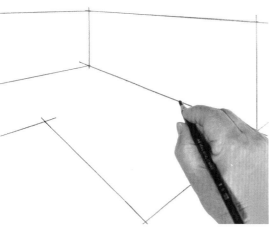

② Trace the template to create lines for the walls and floor

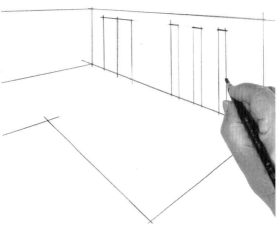

③ Draw a sliding window and slit windows

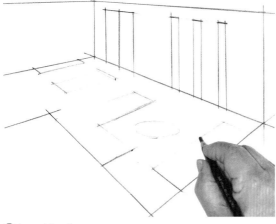

④ Layout furniture

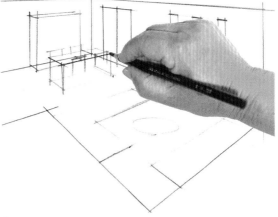

⑤ Draw a china cabinet and a dining set

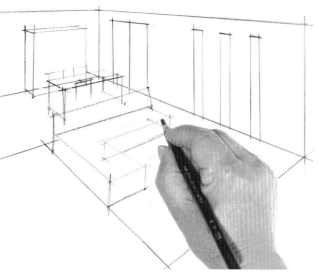

⑥ Draw a sofa

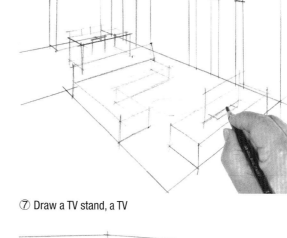

⑦ Draw a TV stand, a TV

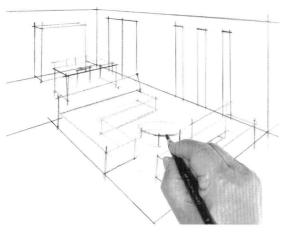

⑧ Draw a coffee table

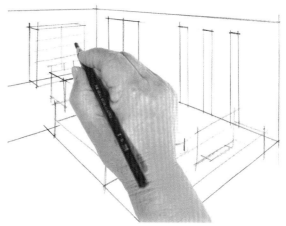

⑨ Draw shelving

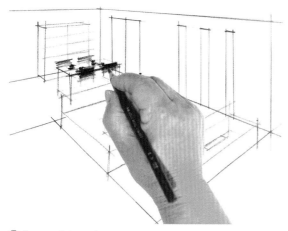

⑩ Draw a dining set

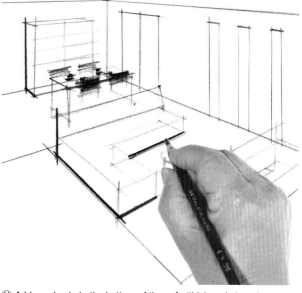

⑪ Add emphasis to the bottom of the sofa (thick and strong)

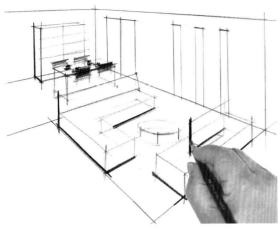

⑫ Add emphasis to the TV stand (thick and strong)

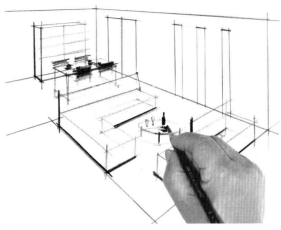

⑬ Draw dishes, etc.

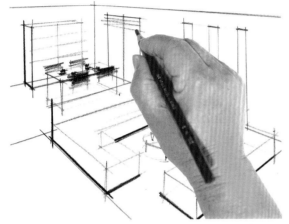

⑭ Add blinds

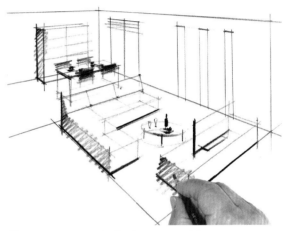

⑮ Cast shadows on the furniture to complete

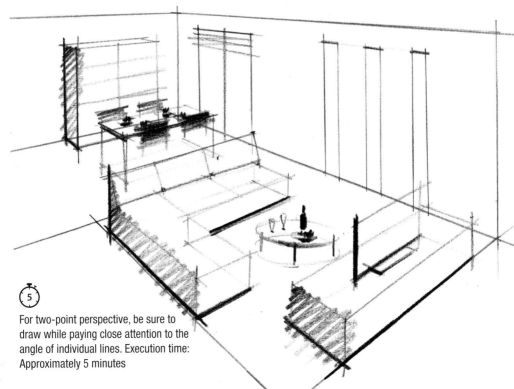

For two-point perspective, be sure to draw while paying close attention to the angle of individual lines. Execution time: Approximately 5 minutes

Chapter 3

Key Points for Drawing

In this chapter, we introduce methods for adding rich expressions to a sketch utilizing simple techniques, such as emphasizing lines and shading.

Living Image Sketch

Varying Lineweight

Adding accents to your lines allows for rich expressions inside your simplified sketches. For sketches that are used simply as a means of communication, it is best to use a pencil that is capable of drawing thick, strong lines in order to clearly convey your ideas to your clients.

Peel-off oil-based pencil (Dermatograph Mitsubishi No. 7600).
The lead of this pencil rarely breaks and you can draw on materials other than paper (glass, plastics, etc.). Thus, it is a very useful tool.

Methods for varying lineweight. First off, if you can draw lines in three different lineweights—fine, medium, and outline—that should be sufficient. However, if you can draw lines in five different lineweights, you will have more than enough. Interestingly, you can see that, on the facing page, convincing sketches can be drawn with just two different lineweights. Hold your pencil gently and draw as if you were just barely supporting it. That enables you to draw pale, thin, and weak lines. On the other hand, holding your pencil firmly and pressing down at an angle forcefully enables you to draw thick and strong lines.

Your shading will be truly smooth if you can control the density of your lines, as well as the pressure of your pencil strokes. This allows your shading to move from strong and thick to thin and pale. Drawing speedily makes for more beautiful shading than drawing slowly.

Conversely, we need to also practice drawing continuous fine shading using lines that go from thin and pale to strong and thick. Once you master this, your range of expression will broaden greatly.

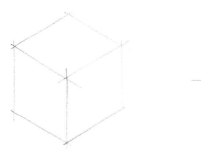

Varied lineweights in a cube. Draw fairly lightly

Outline the bottom two lines of the cube and the perpendicular line on right

Varied lineweights on a bed. Draw fairly lightly

Outline the bottom two lines of the bed and the perpendicular line on the right

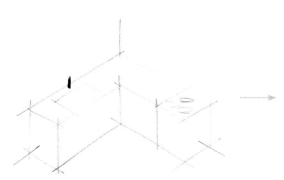

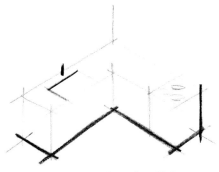

Varied lineweights on a kitchen counter. Draw fairly lightly, except for the faucet

Outline the bottom two lines of the kitchen counter and the perpendicular line on right

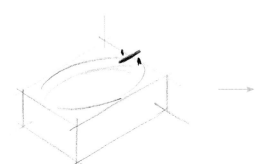

Varied lineweights on a bathtub. Draw fairly lightly, except for the faucet

Outline the bottom two lines of the bathtub and the perpendicular line on the right

Let's practice drawing interior spaces using varying lineweights.
Outline the lines depending on the direction of the light source.

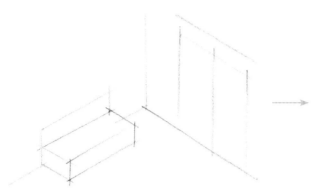

Lightly draw the overall layout of the interior space

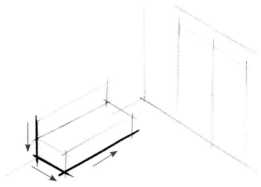

Since the window is on the right side, outline the bottom of the sofa and the perpendicular line on the left

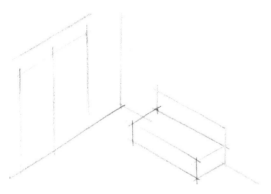

Lightly draw the overall layout of the interior space

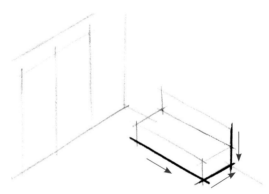

Since the window is on left side, outline the bottom of the sofa and the perpendicular line on the right

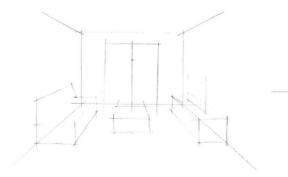

In cases where the window is at the center of the room, just lightly draw the entire interior space

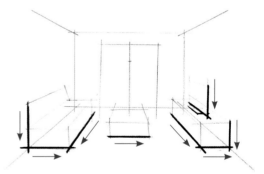

For the sofa, outline the perpendicular line on the left. Also, outline the perpendicular line on the TV stand and the bottom of the coffee table

Add Shading

Through shading, the three-dimensional feel of the object will increase.

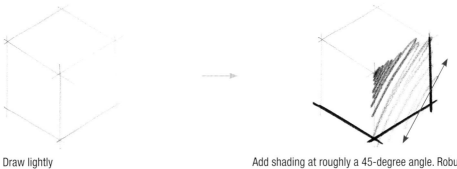

Draw lightly

Add shading at roughly a 45-degree angle. Robustly draw lines that jut out from the edges

■ Bed

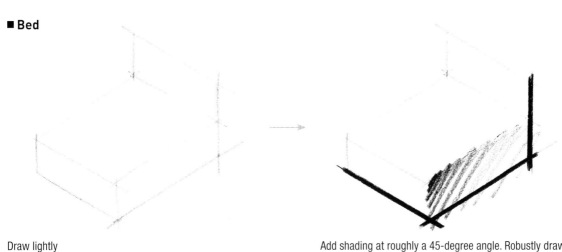

Draw lightly

Add shading at roughly a 45-degree angle. Robustly draw lines that jut out from the edges

■ Bathroom

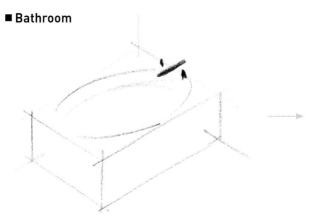

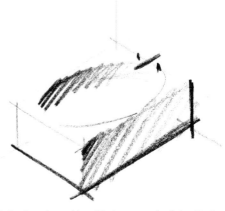

Draw lightly, except for the faucet

Add shading at roughly a 45-degree angle. Robustly draw lines that jut out from the edges

Add Shading

■ Kitchen

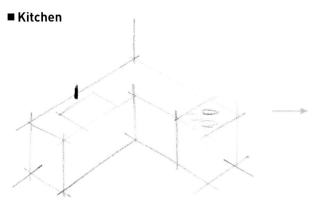

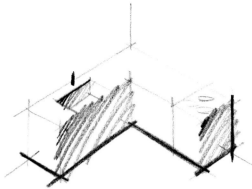

Draw lightly, except for the faucet

Add shading at roughly a 45-degree angle. Robustly draw lines that jut out from the edges

■ Washstand (one-point perspective)

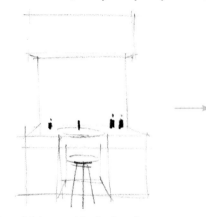

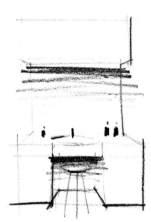

Draw lightly, except for the faucet

Add shading to the mirror and for shadows

■ China cabinet (one-point perspective)

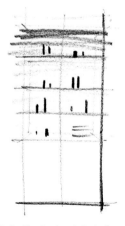

Draw lightly, except for the tableware

Add shading horizontally to the extent that the tableware is somewhat visible. Robustly draw lines with jutting edges

■ Dining Table Set

① Lightly draw a dining table

② Draw four chairs

③ Outline the edge of the table top

④ Outline the foot of the table

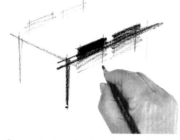

⑤ Add shading. Dark at the forefront, pale at the rear

⑥ Draw plates

⑦ Draw dishes on the plates

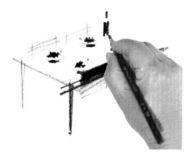

⑧ Draw a bottle of wine to complete

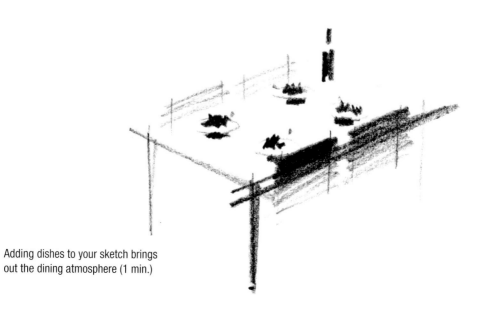

Adding dishes to your sketch brings out the dining atmosphere (1 min.)

■ Livingroom Area

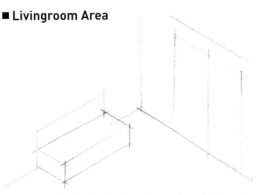

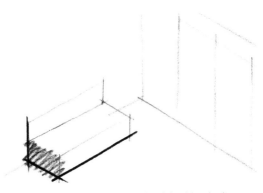

Living room design sketch: Monotonous lineweights and no shading

Since the window is located on the right side, shadows are cast on the left side of the sofa

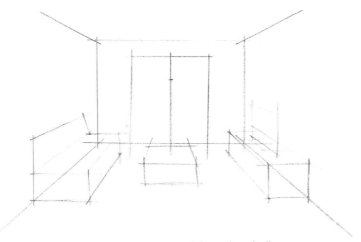

Living room design sketch: Monotonous lineweights and no shading

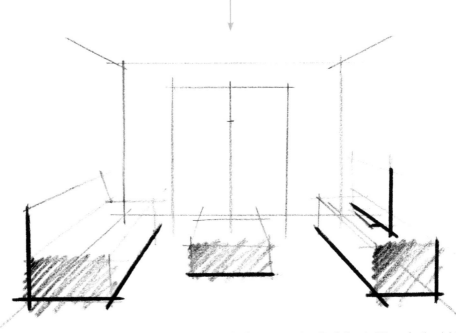

Since the window is located in the middle of the wall, shadows are cast on the left end of the sofa, the right end of the TV stand, and the face of the coffee table. Add shading that robustly juts out. The robustness and swiftness of the lines here creates a certain amount of tastefulness

Applying Varying Lineweights:
Let's Draw Chairs with Iconic Designs

Delicately modifying things while attempting to draw chairs designed by famous designers can result in something quite different from the original. When drawing during conversations with your client you can convey the idea of a certain chair even if that chair is overly simple. In addition, knowing the simplified form of these chairs enables you to draw detailed sketches at a later time relatively easily.

Proposed layout of a living room with chairs (approx. 4min.)

Proposed layout: Colored interior design sketch (drawing + 3 min., total of 7 min.)

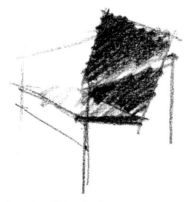

Draw by utilizing shading

Draw by making use of distinctive design features

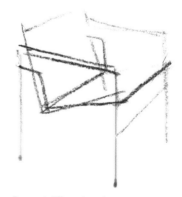

Draw at different angles

■ A – Let's simplify

① Draw the back of a chair

② Draw a seat

③ Draw armrests

④ Draw three legs of a chair, then the simplified form is complete

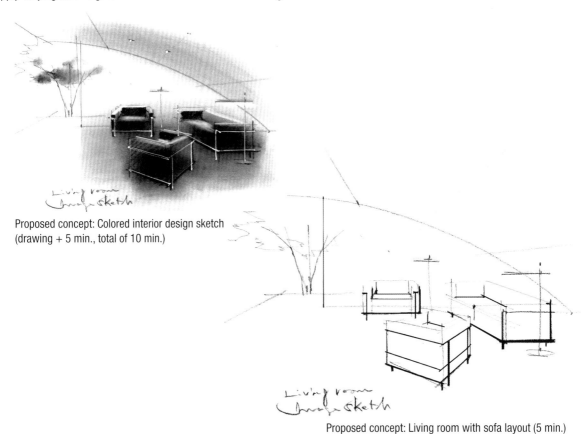

Proposed concept: Colored interior design sketch
(drawing + 5 min., total of 10 min.)

Proposed concept: Living room with sofa layout (5 min.)

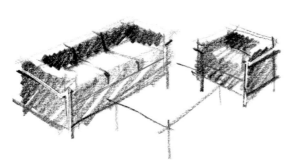

Draw by utilizing shading

Draw by making use of distinctive design features (drawn with a fountain pen)

Example from a different angle: From the top

■ B – Let's simplify

① Create the broad image of an upper plane

② Capture the overall image of a chair

③ Mark the seat of the chair

④ Completed rough draft of overall image of a chair

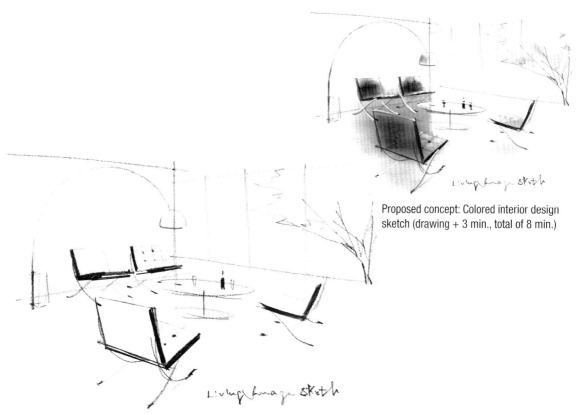

Proposed concept: Colored interior design sketch (drawing + 3 min., total of 8 min.)

Proposed concept: Living room with a chair layout (5 min.)

Draw by making use of shading

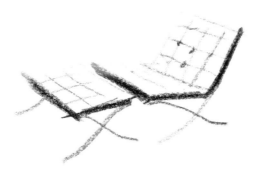

Draw by making use of distinctive design features

■ C – Let's simplify

① Draw the back of a chair

② Draw a seat

③ Draw the curved legs of a chair

④ Draw the rest of the legs to complete your rough draft

START!!

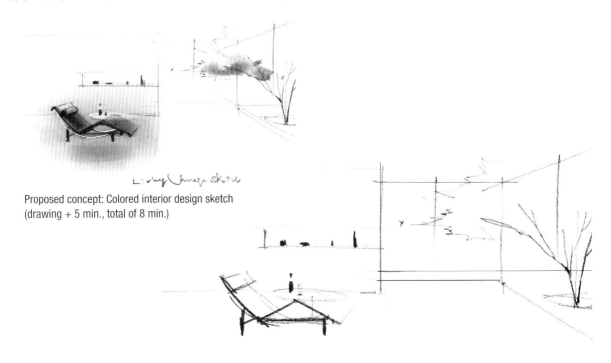

Proposed concept: Colored interior design sketch
(drawing + 5 min., total of 8 min.)

Proposed concept: Living room with sofa layout
(approx. 3 min.)

Draw by making use of shading

Draw by making use of
distinctive design features
(drawn with a fountain pen)

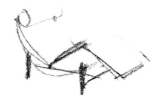

Draw different angles

■ D – Let's simplify

① Capture the rough
image of a sideline of
a chair

② Draw a seat, etc.

③ Add a
headrest

④ Draw the curved
line of the frame

⑤ Draw the legs to
complete your rough
draft

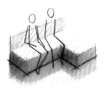

Chapter 4

Key Points for Coloring

This chapter will introduce coloring methods for flooring and furniture, as well as techniques for rendering light and shadow. Materials used are: Color pencils (six colors), pastels, kneaded erasers, and white-out. When light and shadow are added through coloring, even simplified interior design sketches experience an increased sense of "presence".

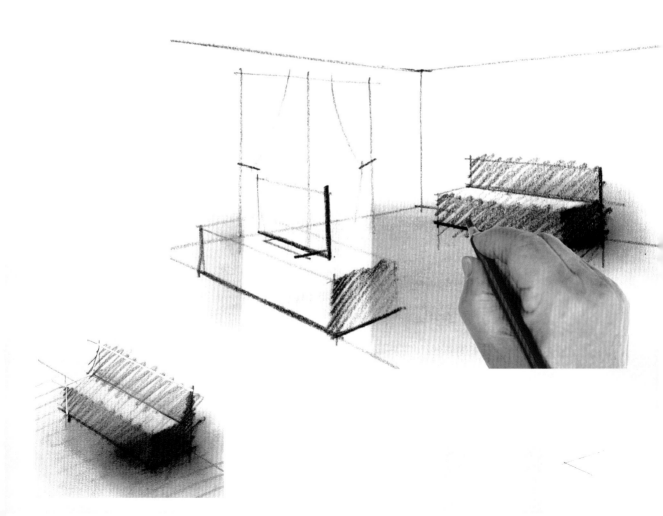

Coloring Basics

Even though various coloring materials are available for interior design sketches, we must remember that, for communication sketches, we need to maintain the ability to respond at a moment's notice. As a result of various attempts to achieve both speed and quality, I have come to the conclusion that it is best to use pastels for foundations (floors, walls, etc.), color pencils for furniture and small objects, and a kneaded eraser for light and shadow. Also, use white-out to accentuate brightness and light. Use these materials as suggested to create effective and speedy communication sketches.

As far as paper is concerned, the ordinary store bought kind will do. Commercially available A4 (letter) sized copier paper, the three basic colored pastels, and a few additional colors should be sufficient for responding to your client's needs at an initial consultation stage.

Six colored pencils in different colors should be sufficient. Despite your best efforts to faithfully reproduce colors chosen by your client, it will actually be impossible to match the colors exactly because the paper will end up washing out your colors. Instead of thinking, "this is the color", you should strive to collectively achieve "an atmosphere that is something like this".

Different types of pastels are available commercially. For your reference, I should mention that I use semi-hard pastels from "Holbein".

For speedsketching, six different color pencils will do the job. Dermatograph oil-based pencils in red, green, and navy can be used instead of simple color pencils.

A kneaded eraser is indispensable for rendering light.

White-out is a must for accentuating light (Pentel Presto Fine-tip).

Color floors mainly with pastels. To create a beautiful finish, apply brown pastel to a white pastel foundation that you first blended with your fingertips.

Directly laying down brown pastel without first applying the white foundation will result in unevenness, as you can see here.

■ Let's try some techniques with a sofa

① Attempt to draw a sofa

② Apply white pastel as the foundation

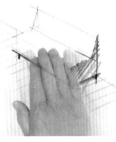

③ Move your fingertips horizontally across the paper to blend

④ Apply floor color (brown)

⑤ Gently blend the floor color onto the base. Don't worry if you color the sofa a bit

⑥ Apply black for shadows

⑦ Blend with your fingertips

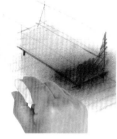

⑧ Create bright portions of the floor with a kneaded eraser (simply erase the pastels you applied)

⑨ Render the seat of the sofa with a kneaded eraser

⑩ Color the sofa with a color pencil. Lightly apply color to the entire sofa

⑪ Color the back and base of the sofa slightly darker

⑫ Color the side of the sofa darker, more thick, and more dense

⑬ Add accents to bright areas on the sofa with white-out to complete

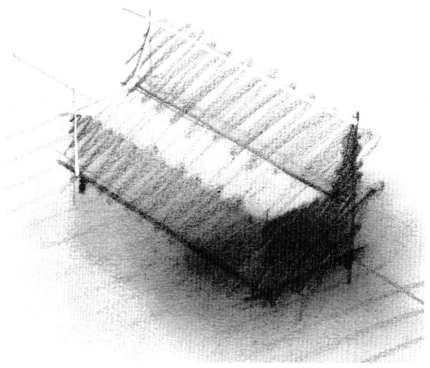

Execution time: Approximately 3 minutes

Let's Render Window Reflections 1

This section deals with rendering "reflections on a floor from a bright area" of the window, instead of "sun light" from the window. As seen in the presentation drawing on the right, the reflection is not from light coming in at an angle through the window. Rather, similar to a mirror, the "windows" themselves, along with other areas of brightness, are vertically reflected on the floor. Doing this allows the quality of the floor finish to be conveyed. Make a photocopy of the one-point perspective guide on P.155 and lay it under paper to help you gauge perspective balance.

Here is a sample presentation of reflections from a window (*Sketching Interiors: Color* by Yoshinori Hasegawa)

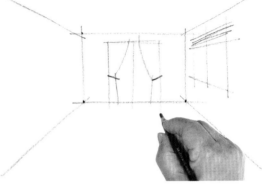

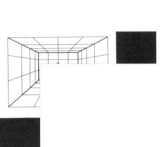

① Place a piece of A4 (letter) sized paper on the copied one-point perspective guide

② Draw the "sliding window" and "bay window" on the right wall

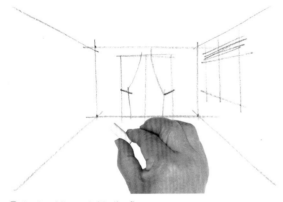

③ Apply white pastel to the floor

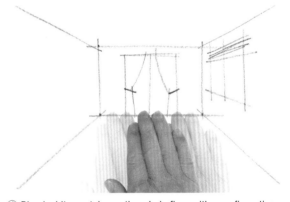

④ Blend white pastel over the whole floor with your fingertips

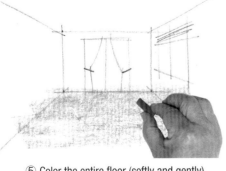

⑤ Color the entire floor (softly and gently) with your chosen floor color (usually brown)

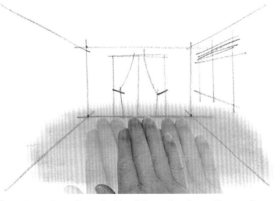

⑥ Horizontally, and evenly, blend the entire floor with your fingers

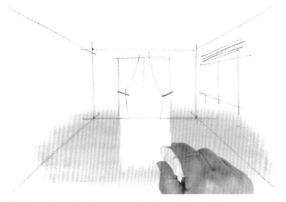

⑦ Using a kneaded eraser, render the sliding window reflections on the floor

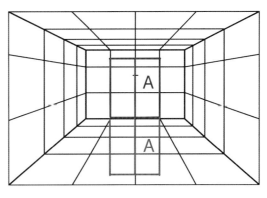

With a kneaded eraser, erase reflections on floor "A (blue)" at the same height as the sliding window "A (red)"

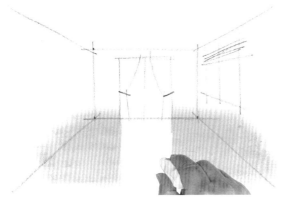

⑧ Originally, "A" has the same dimension as the sliding window. However, this time I decided to erase up to the edge. Doing so speeds up the process because it is not necessary to measure everything

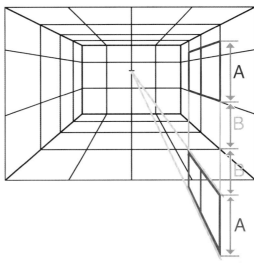

The height of the bay window is "A (red)" and "B" is the height of the floor from the bay window. Notice that "A (blue)" is the same height as "A (red)". Erase "A (blue)" with a kneaded eraser

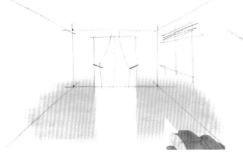

⑨ To complete, simply render the reflection of the bay window using a kneaded eraser

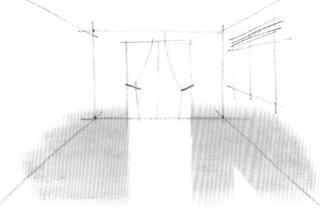

Don't worry about rendering the reflection of the curtain. Execution time: Approximately 2 minutes

Let's Render Window Reflections 2

In two-point perspective there will be a reflection on the floor directly below each window. Make a photocopy of the two-point perspective guide on P.156 and lay it under a piece of paper to help you to gauge perspective.

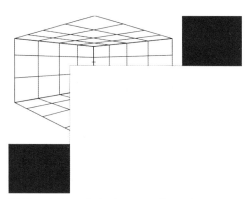

① Place A4 (letter) sized paper on the copied two-point perspective guide

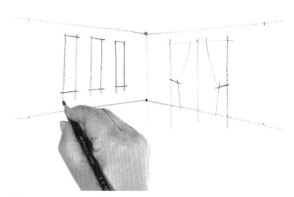

② Draw "slit windows" on the left wall, and "sliding windows" on the right wall

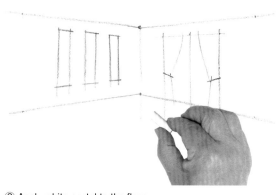

③ Apply white pastel to the floor

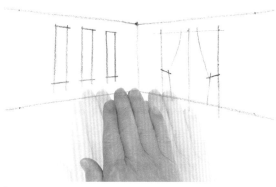

④ Blend the white pastel over whole floor with your fingertips

⑤ Softly and gently color the entire floor brown

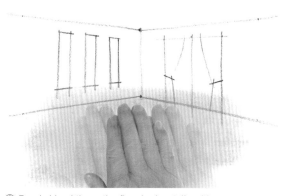

⑥ Evenly blend the entire floor horizontally with your fingers

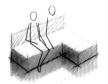

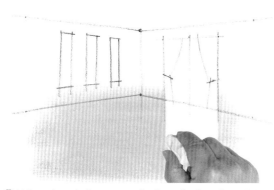

⑦ Using a kneaded eraser, render the reflection of the sliding window on the floor

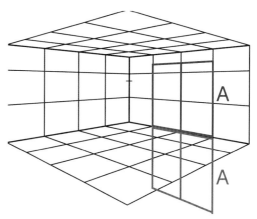

With a kneaded eraser, erase reflection on the floor "A (blue)" to the same size as the sliding window "A (red)"

⑧ Using a kneaded eraser, render the reflection of the slit window on the floor to complete

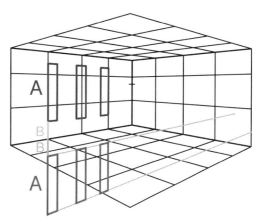

The height of the slit window is "A (red)". "B (yellow)" is the height from the floor to the bottom of the slit window. With a kneaded eraser, erase a reflection on the floor that is the same dimension as "A (red)" + "B (yellow)". The "A (blue)" portion is the reflection

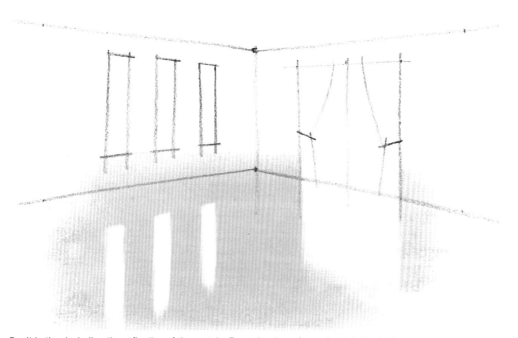

Don't bother including the reflection of the curtain. Execution time: Approximately 3 minutes

Let's Render Window Reflections 3 Coloring Floors and Furniture

Let's practice coloring with a living room that has a very simple composition. Make a photocopy of the two-point perspective guide on P.156 and lay it under paper to help you gauge perspective balance.

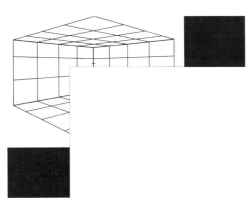

① Place A4 (letter) sized paper on the copied two-point perspective guide

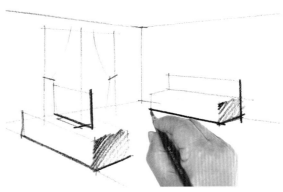

② Complete drawing (approx. 2 min.)

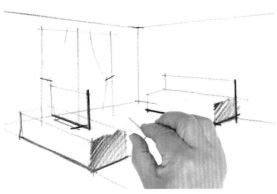

③ Color the floor with white pastel

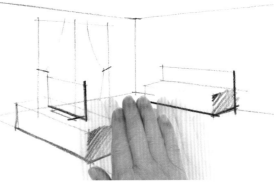

④ Use your fingers to blend white pastel over the whole floor

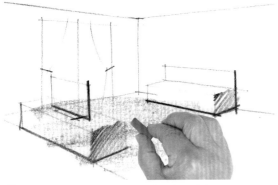

⑤ Color the entire floor brown (soft and gentle)

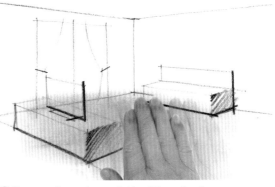

⑥ Use your fingers to evenly blend the entire floor horizontally

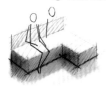

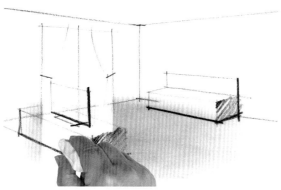

⑦ Create the reflection of the sliding window using a kneaded eraser

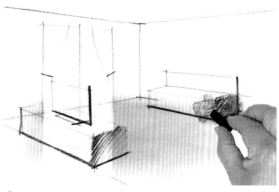

⑧ Add shadows with black pastel

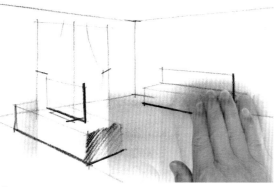

⑨ Smudge the shadow with your fingers (broadly)

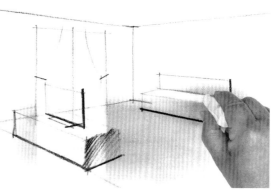

⑩ Erase pastels on the seat of the sofa with a kneaded eraser

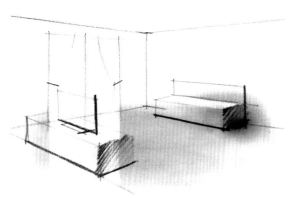

⑪ It is fine to finish at this point

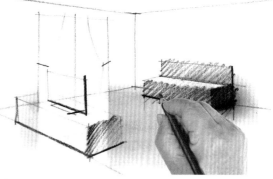

⑫ Color the sofa with color pencils to complete

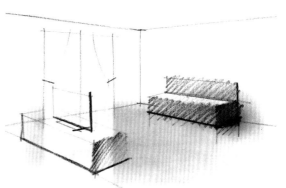

Execution time: Approximately 5 minutes

Indirect Lighting 1
Drawing a Living Room

Let's render indirect lighting effects, etc., using pastels, a kneaded eraser, and white-out. Since this is just practice for lighting effects, I have purposely planned to use less colors. Make a photocopy of the one-point perspective guide on P.155 and lay it under some paper to helps you gauge balanced perspective.

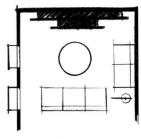

Living room floor plan

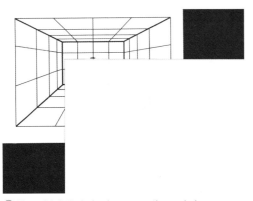

① Place A4 (letter) sized paper on the copied one-point perspective guide

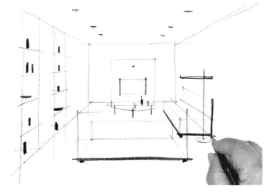

② Completed living room (approx. 3 min.)

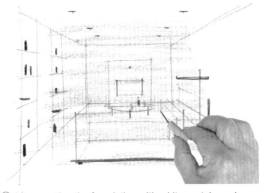

③ After creating the foundation with white pastel, overlay gray

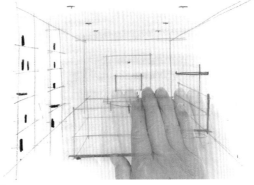

④ Evenly blend the pastels using your fingertips. Make the shelves on the left bright by using a kneaded eraser

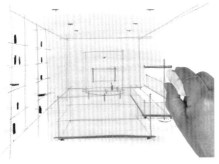

⑤ Use a kneaded eraser to render the seat of the sofa and the floor lamp lighting

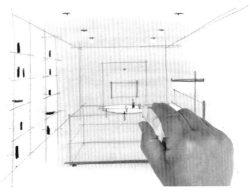

⑥ Render some downlights and a coffee table

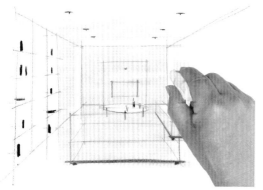

⑦ Brighten the indirect lighting on the facing wall using a kneaded eraser

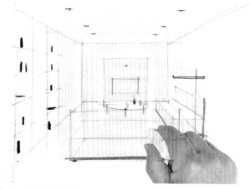

⑧ Brighten the indirect lighting in the foreground and on both side walls using a kneaded eraser (include the reflection on the floor)

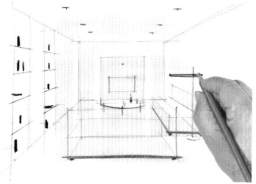

⑨ Color the shade of the lamp, the edges of the coffee table, and the edges of the shelving with a green pencil

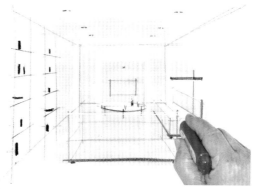

⑩ Render the brightest part of the downlights on the ceiling, the sofa, and the coffee table using a white-out

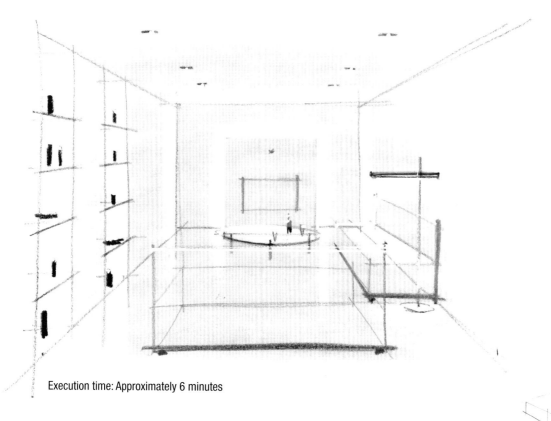

Execution time: Approximately 6 minutes

Indirect Lighting 2
Drawing a Bedroom with an Arched Ceiling

Into the gentle atmosphere brought out by the arched ceiling, we will insert some indirect lighting and downlights. This layout includes portions that will utilize kneaded eraser techniques. For example, rendering indirect lighting effects on the headboard of the bed. Additionally, pastels will be blended, not only with our fingertips but also with facial tissue, to achieve a beautiful finish without any unevenness in the coloring. Make a photocopy of the one-point perspective guide on P.155 and lay it under some paper to help gauge perspective.

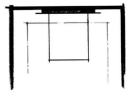

Simple bedroom floor plan

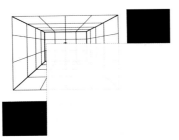

① Place A4 (letter) sized paper on the copied one-point perspective guide

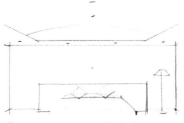

② Complete drawing of a bedroom (approx. 3 min.)

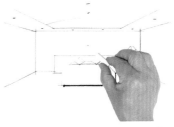

③ Color everything with white pastel

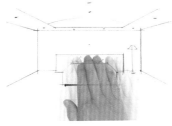

④ Blend the overall surface with your fingertips

⑤ Color the entire surface light brown

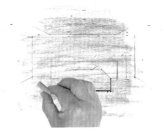

⑥ Add gray in order to mute the color

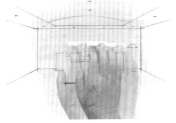

⑦ Blend everything in with facial tissue (for large areas)

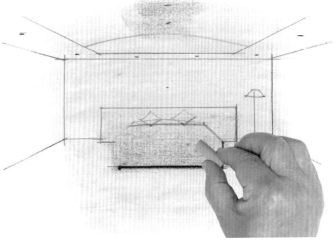

⑧ Add shadows to the ceiling and the bed with gray (to emphasize depth)

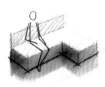

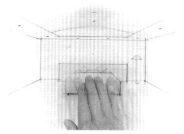

⑨ Blend with fingertips

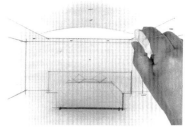

⑩ Use a kneaded eraser to add lighting effects on the ceiling

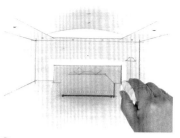

⑪ Add light around the headboard of the bed with a kneaded eraser

⑫ Add light to the floor stand with a kneaded eraser

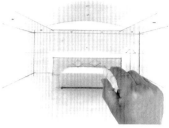

⑬ Add light to the top of the bed with a kneaded eraser

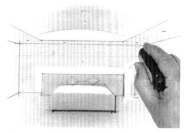

⑭ Draw downlights using white-out to complete

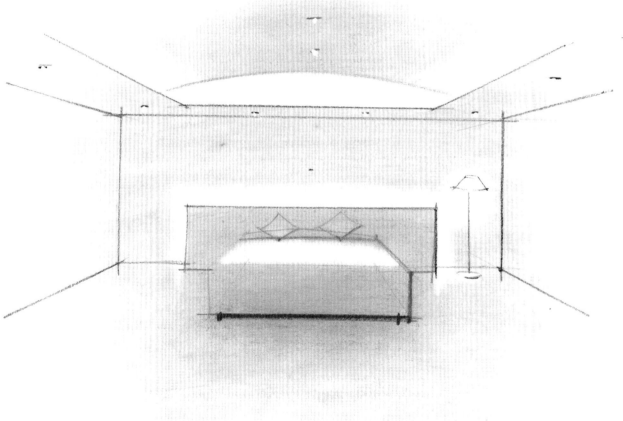

Execution time: Approximately 7 minutes

Key Points for Rendering Light and Shadows

The key points visible here include expressing shadows using pastels and rendering brightness using a kneaded eraser.

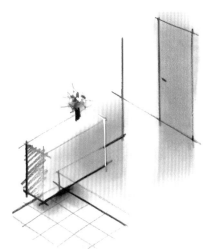

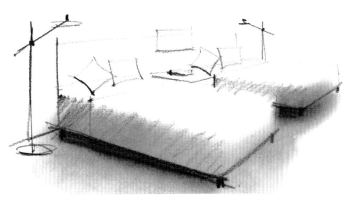

For the mattress here, you just erase the pastels on top with a kneaded eraser

Reflections added to a hallway with a kneaded eraser

Add brightness on the sofa seat with a kneaded eraser to finish. As for the floor, color with pastels first then take out the sofa reflections using a kneaded eraser

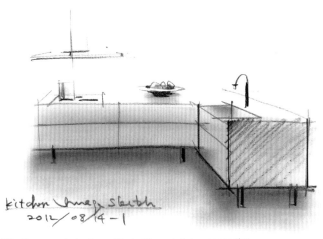

Effective use of shading added with pastels increases the "presence" of the kitchen counter

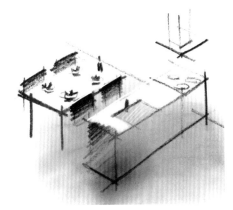

A certain clean appeal is created by erasing pastels on the counter-top and the tabletop

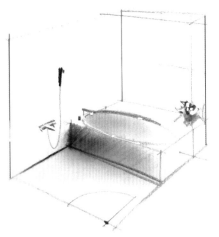

As for the bathtub, erase the edges to bring about a clear and bright look

Chapter 5

Speedsketch Presentation

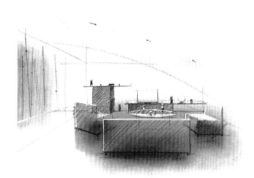

This chapter simulates sketches drawn at a meeting with a client in order to exhibit the practical application of speedsketch methods introduced up to this point. The objective here is to create communication sketches while having a conversation with a client.

⑦ [7 Minute Sketch] Bathroom Area

Use transparent lines in order to clearly present both the layout and the flowing lines of a bathroom.

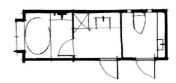

A lengthwise layout plan of a bathroom area

① Begin by drawing isometric projections. Lightly draw the floor with a dermatograph pencil

② Build up a wall encasing the bathroom area

③ Eyeball the size of each space and partition them

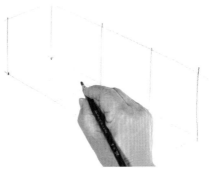

④ Begin to draw the bathroom. At first, layout the bathtub and shower area

⑤ Draw a bathroom door

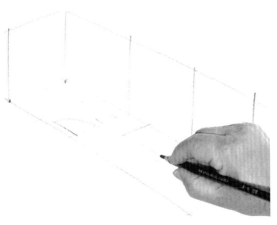

⑥ Layout a washer and a washstand

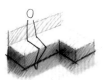

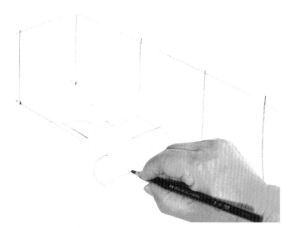

⑦ Draw a utility room door

⑧ Layout a toilet

⑨ Add the position of a washroom door and a washstand

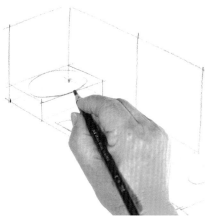

⑩ Draw a three-dimensional bathtub

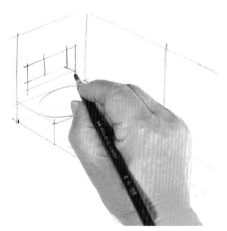

⑪ Draw a bay window in the bathroom

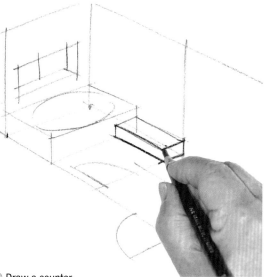

⑫ Draw a counter

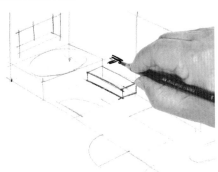

⑬ Draw a multifunctional faucet

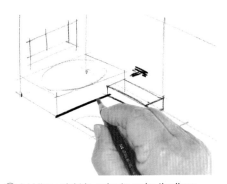

⑭ Add lineweight in order to make the lines easier to see

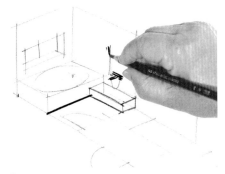

⑮ Draw a shower-head

⑯ Draw a mirror to complete the bathroom

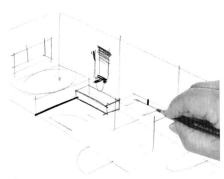

⑰ Draw a washstand

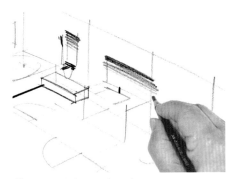

⑱ Add gradations to the mirror

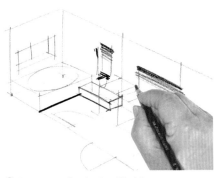

⑲ Draw a washer in simplified form

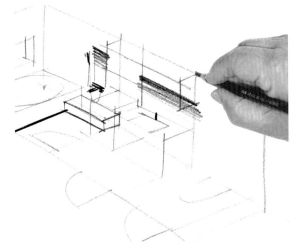

⑳ Draw a simplified bathroom cabinet

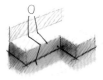

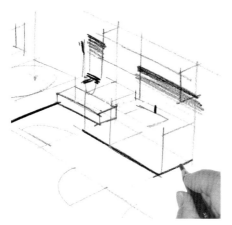

㉑ Emphasize the lines of the powder room (make the lines that touch the floor darker, thicker, and stronger). The powder room is complete

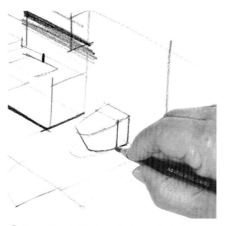

㉒ According to the layout, draw a tank-less type toilet

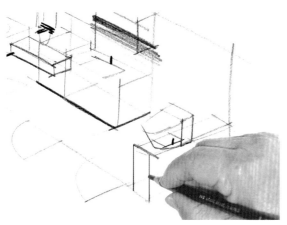

㉓ Add a washroom counter

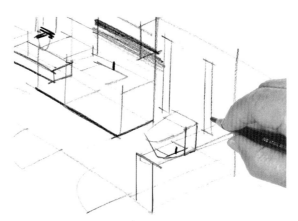

㉔ Draw in some slit windows. The washroom is complete

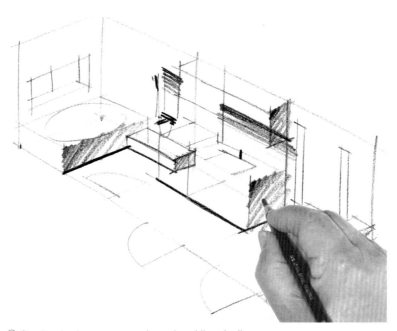

㉕ Our drawing becomes even clearer by adding shading

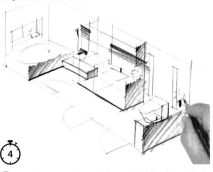

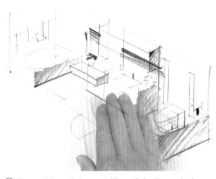

㉖ Add plants to the window sill of the bay window, to the bathroom counter, and to the washroom counter. The pencil drawing is complete at this point. If you don't have time to add color, just present your drawing as is. (up to here takes approx. 4 min.)

㉗ From this point, we will explain the coloring process. First off, apply white pastel to create the foundation

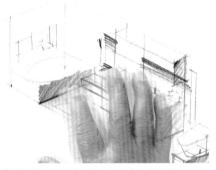

㉘ Shadows can be nicely rendered just by rubbing the shading down from the bathtub

㉙ Given that the bathroom counter and washroom floor are intended to be made from wood we need to color them with brown pastel

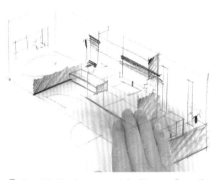

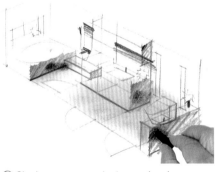

㉚ Blend in the brown pastel with your fingertips

㉛ Shadows can accentuate any drawing so we need to add black after choosing the portions that need to be darkened. Be careful to rein in your shading to prevent the entire drawing from becoming dark

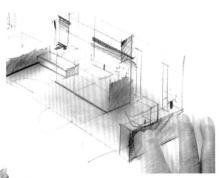

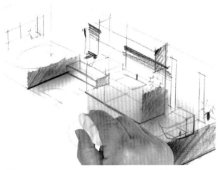

㉜ Blend in with your fingertips

㉝ Erase areas you intend to make bright

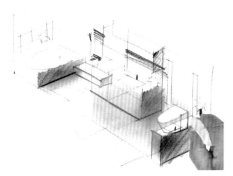

㉞ Make the top of the washroom counter and the top of the toilet brighter using a kneaded eraser. The overall image has sharpened quite a bit

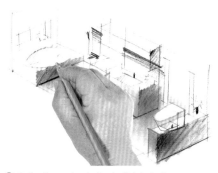

㉟ Color the water in the bathtub, bathroom sink, and washroom sink

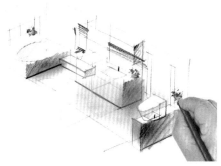

㊱ Color the flowers in each of the three different areas (red and green)

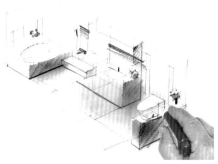

㊲ Use white-out to render brightness and place accents in your drawing to complete

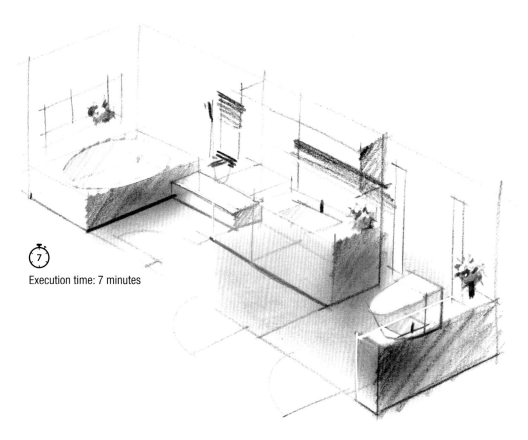

⏱ 7
Execution time: 7 minutes

⑦ [7 Minute Sketch]
A House where a Married Couple Happily Lives

This section introduces the approach for composing an isometric projection sketch from a floor plan. I named this approach "origami sketching" because the floor plan is drawn on a creased piece of paper. This is a very practical sketching method that can be used in the presence of your client. As an example, we will use a senior citizen's style living, dining, and kitchen space.

A - Hold the right bottom corner of the paper (A4/letter size)

B - Fold the paper diagonally and crease firmly

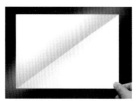

C - Unfold the paper so that the diagonal line is exposed

D - Place the paper at an angle so the creased line appears horizontal. "Origami sketch" prep. is done

① Draw a floor plan

② Return the paper to its horizontal position, thus angling the floor plan

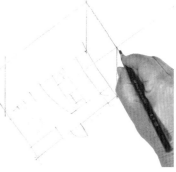

③ Draw the walls that encase the floor while paying attention to ceiling height

④ Add a window to the wall

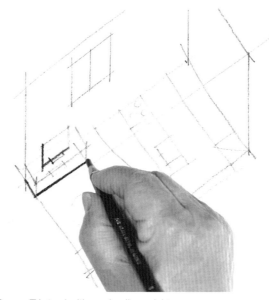

⑤ Draw a TV stand with varying lineweight

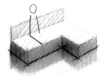

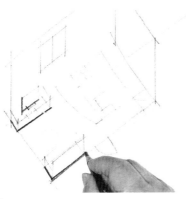

⑥ Draw a sofa

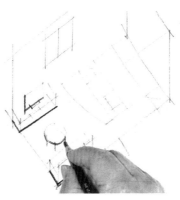

⑦ Draw a coffee table

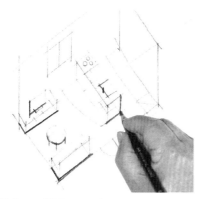

⑧ Draw a kitchen counter

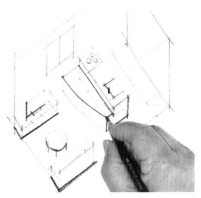

⑨ Draw a dining table

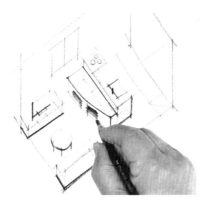

⑩ Draw two chairs

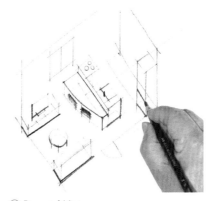

⑪ Draw a fridge

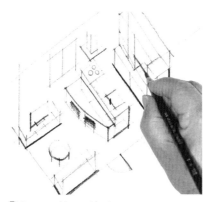

⑫ Draw a china cabinet

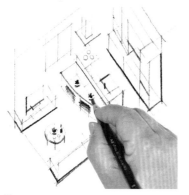

⑬ Draw dishes

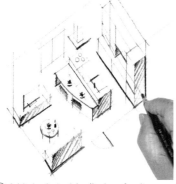

⑭ Add shadows (shading) on furniture and appliances

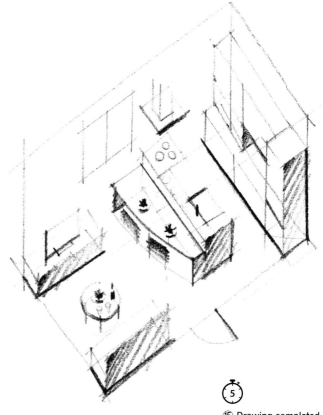

⑮ Drawing completed. So far we have taken about 5 min.

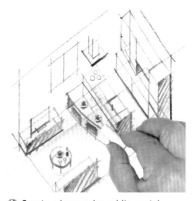

⑯ Create a base using white pastel

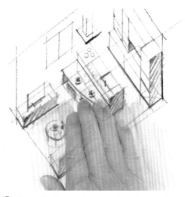

⑰ Smooth the white pastel with your fingertips where you intend to color the floor

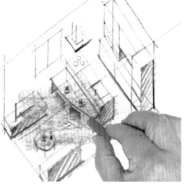

⑱ Color the floor using a brown pastel

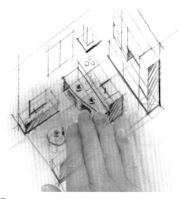

⑲ Smooth out the brown pastel evenly with fingertips

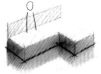

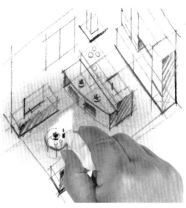

⑳ Erase pastels with a kneaded eraser as you confirm the positions of the window reflections with your eye

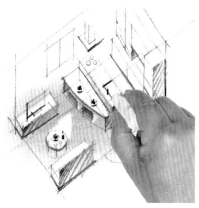

㉑ Brighten the surface of the kitchen counter, TV stand, sofa, and tabletop

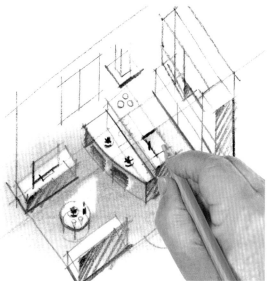
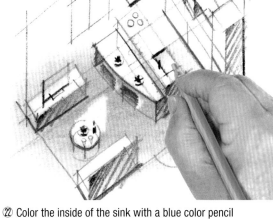

㉒ Color the inside of the sink with a blue color pencil

㉓ Color dishes to complete

For the purpose of initial sketches, the use of color is kept to a minimum as we are attempting to portray things "somewhat like they are" rather than "exactly as they are". Execution time: 7 minutes

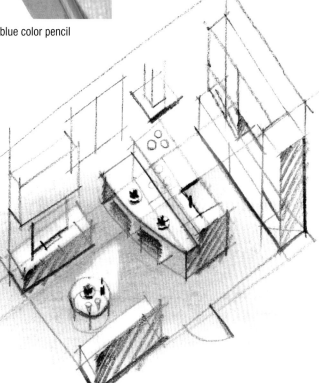

⏱️ (10) [10 Minute Sketch]
A House where Anyone Can Enjoy a Little Tea

This is a single section living, dining, and kitchen space. This floor plan suggests the possibility of enjoying tea at a breakfast bar. When sketching in your client's presence, the key is to limit the use of color because it will allow you to finish quickly. It also reduces the risk of disagreements over differences in color preference.

A - Hold the bottom right corner of the paper (A4/letter size)

B - Fold the paper diagonally so that a diagonal line is creased firmly

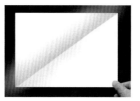

C - Unfold the paper so that the diagonal line appears

D - Angle the paper so that the creased line is horizontal. "Origami sketch" prep. is done

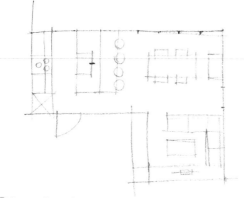

① Draw a floor plan

② Return the paper to horizontal so that the floor plan is now angled

③ Draw lines to build walls that encase the floor while paying attention to the ceiling height

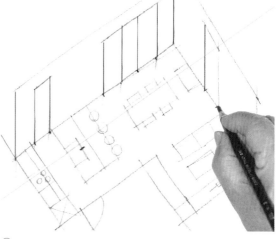

④ Draw a window on the wall

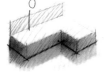

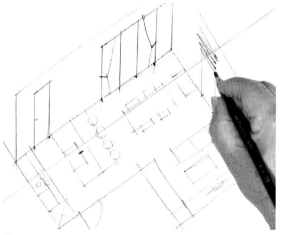

⑤ Draw a curtain

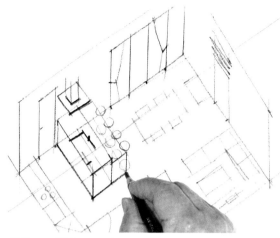

⑥ Draw a kitchen counter

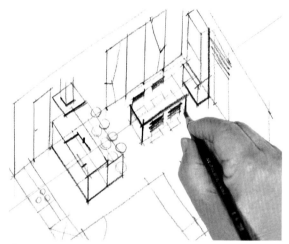

⑦ Draw a china cabinet and a dining table set

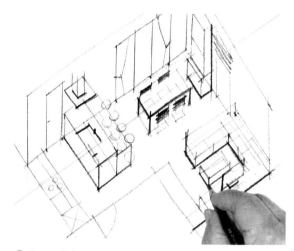

⑧ Draw a living room space by adding a sofa, etc.

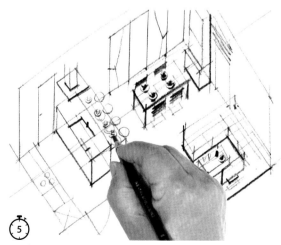

⑨ Draw small items like dishes, etc., to complete. This took approx. 5 min.

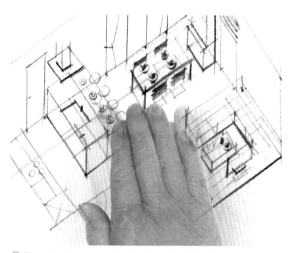

⑩ The coloring process begins here. Create a base for coloring using white pastel

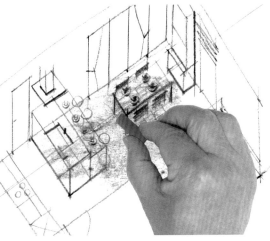

⑪ Color the floor in pastel. Color mainly around the windows

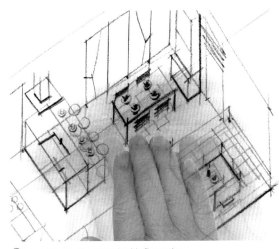

⑫ Smooth out the pastel with fingertips

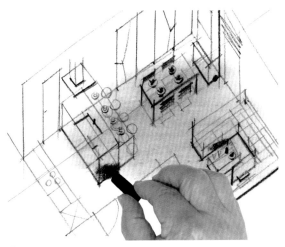

⑬ Add shadows with black pastel (keep it minimal)

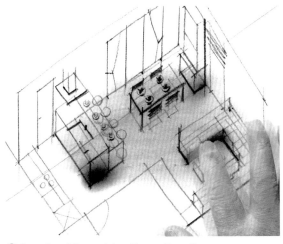

⑭ Smooth out the pastels with your fingertips

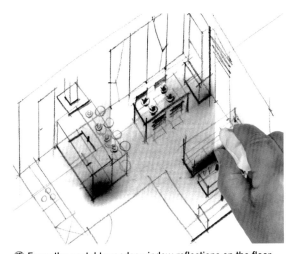

⑮ Erase the pastel to render window reflections on the floor

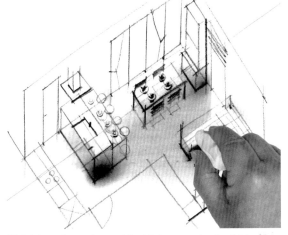

⑯ Brighten the surfaces of the kitchen counter, the table, and the appliances/furniture in the living room with a kneaded eraser

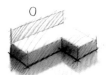

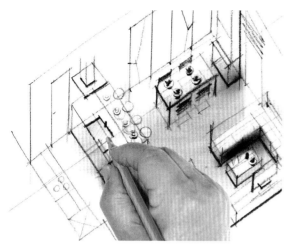

⑰ Color the kitchen sink

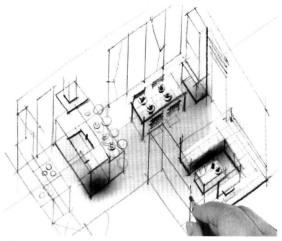

⑱ Use a dermatograph pencil to render the shelf contours

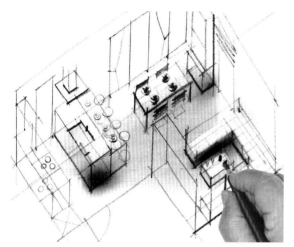

⑲ Color the dishes

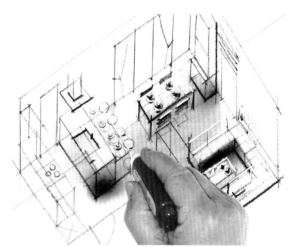

⑳ Add brightness with white-out to complete

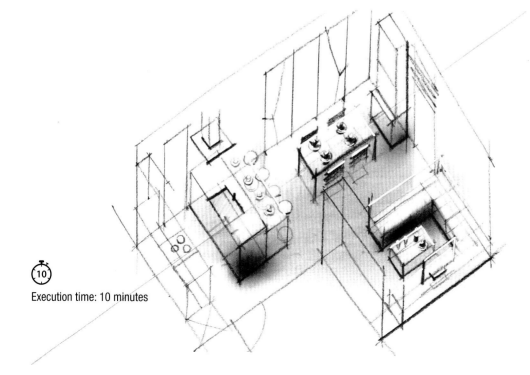

🕙 (10)
Execution time: 10 minutes

⑤ [5 Minute Sketch] Just Lay Back and Enjoy Watching some TV

This is a 157 ft² living room. Draw in one-point perspective.
The layout is a simple composition that consists of a sofa, a TV stand, and a coffee table. The chair in the foreground, placed at an angle, may be slightly challenging to draw, but it shouldn't be a problem if you are diligent in your practice.

Floor plan

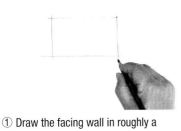

① Draw the facing wall in roughly a 2:3 ratio

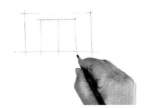

② Draw a sliding window

③ Draw the floor and ceiling lines

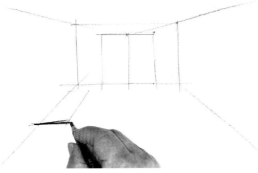

④ Layout your furniture using different lineweights. Begin to draw the TV stand on the left first

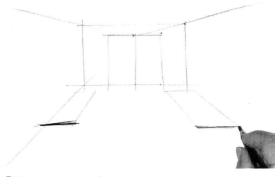

⑤ Next, layout the sofa

⑥ Layout the chair diagonally

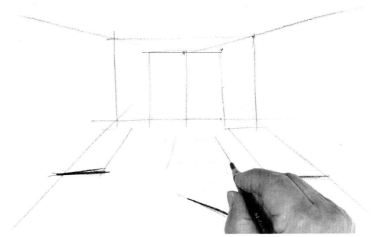

⑦ Lastly, layout your coffee table

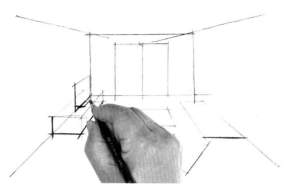

⑧ Draw a TV stand

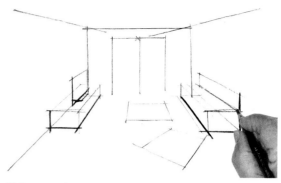

⑨ Draw a sofa

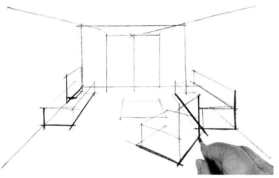

⑩ Draw the diagonally placed chair in the foreground slightly larger than the other furniture, while still paying attention to the overall balance of the living room

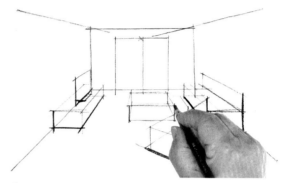

⑪ Draw a coffee table

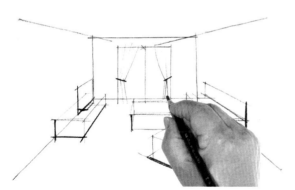

⑫ Draw a curtain. Draw holdbacks strong and add angled wrinkles

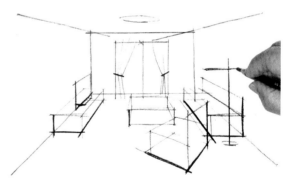

⑬ Draw lights (ceiling lights as well as the floor lamp)

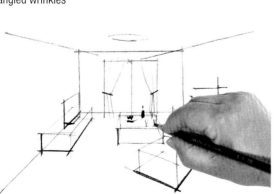

⑭ Draw small objects on the coffee table

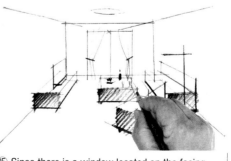

⑮ Since there is a window located on the facing wall we need to add shadows on the near side of the furniture

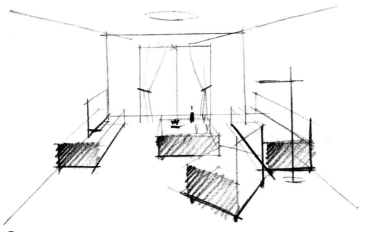

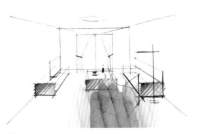

⑯ Drawing complete (3 min.)

⑰ The coloring process can now begin. Create a base with white pastel

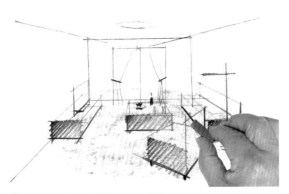

⑱ Color the floor with brown pastel

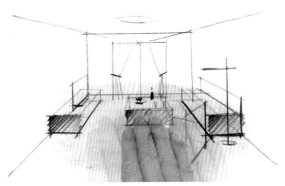

⑲ Smooth out the floor with your fingertips

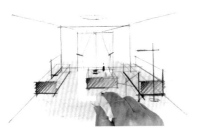

⑳ Render the reflections of the sliding window on the floor with a kneaded eraser

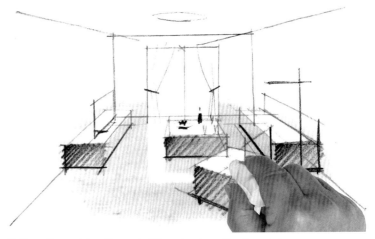

㉑ Erase the pastel on the seat of the sofa, etc., with a kneaded eraser

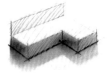

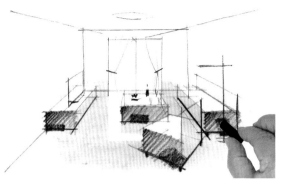
㉒ Add shadows with black pastel

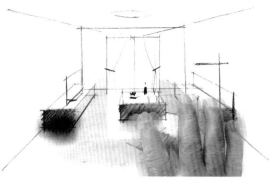
㉓ Smooth out the pastel with your fingertips

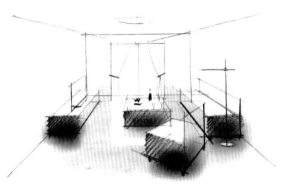
㉔ Almost finished

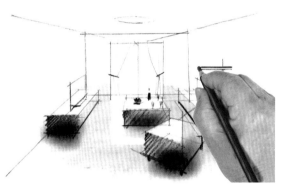
㉕ Use color pencils to color the floor lamp and dishes on the coffee table

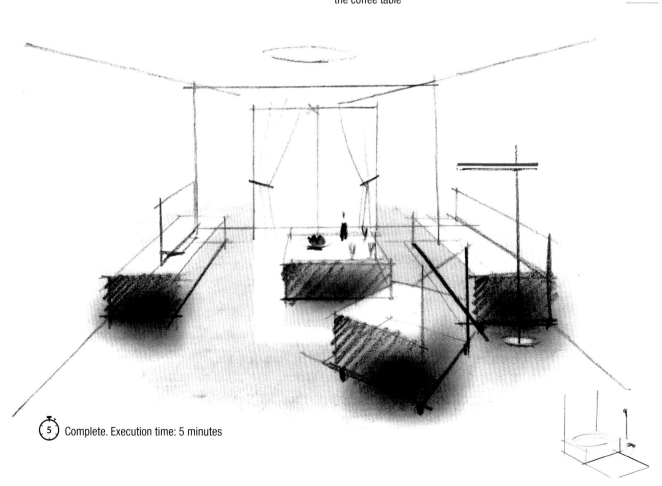
⑤ Complete. Execution time: 5 minutes

⏱️(10) [10 Minute Sketch] An Entryway with Glass Blocks

This section is a 157 ft² entryway. Draw in one-point perspective. Behind the wall of glass blocks is a storage unit. The key point here is adding attractiveness through lighting effects. Also, the use of a kneaded eraser for your coloring techniques is quite important.

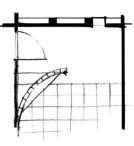

Floor plan

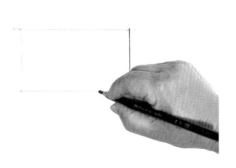

① Draw the facing wall. The aspect ratio for the 157 ft² space is 2:3. Just balance things out roughly

② Draw the guide lines for the wall and floor to create perspective

③ Draw a step

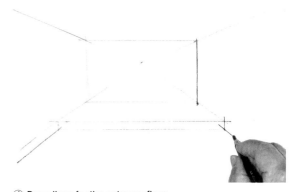

④ Draw lines for the entrance floor

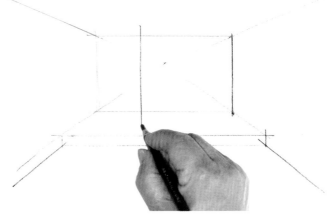

⑤ Draw a line where the wall of glass blocks begins

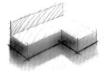

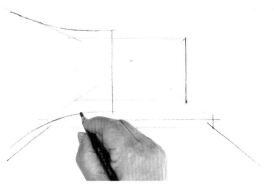

⑥ Draw the curve of the glass block wall by eyeballing it

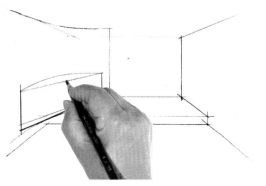

⑦ Draw a storage unit

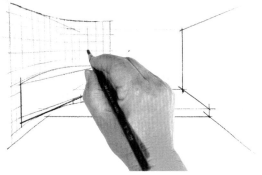

⑧ Though it takes some time, draw in the grout of the glass block wall

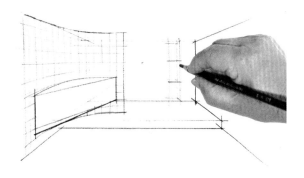

⑨ Add shelving

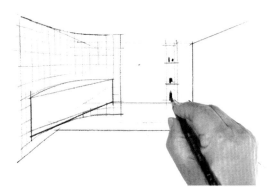

⑩ Draw some display objects on the shelf

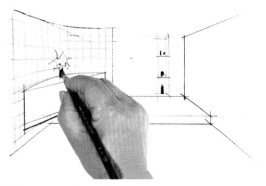

⑪ Draw some flowers in a vase

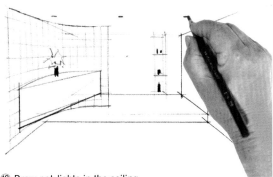

⑫ Draw pot-lights in the ceiling

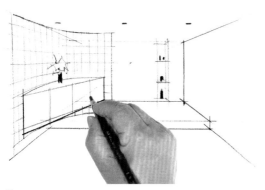

⑬ Draw the lines for the doors on the storage unit

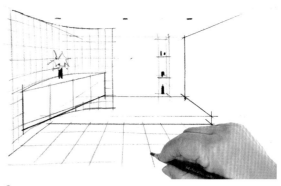

⑭ Draw tiles on the entrance floor

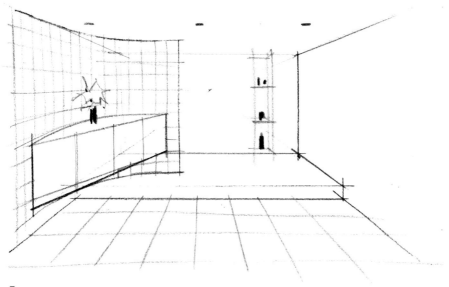

⑮ Your drawing is complete (approx. 5 min.)

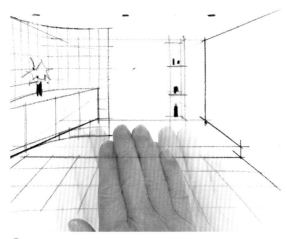

⑱ In preparation for pastel coloring, first evenly apply white pastel

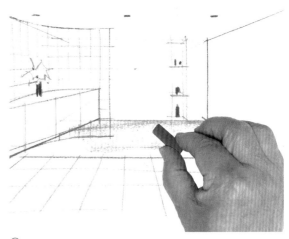

⑰ Color the floor

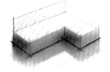

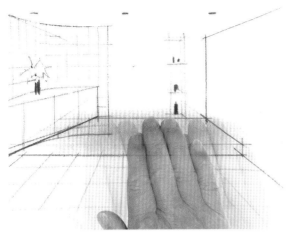

⑱ Smooth out the floor color with your fingertips

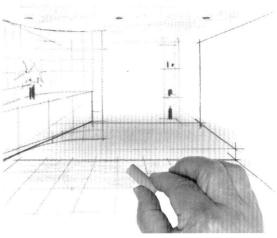

⑲ Color the ceiling and entrance floor gray

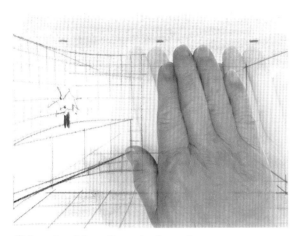

⑳ Smooth out the ceiling and entrance floor

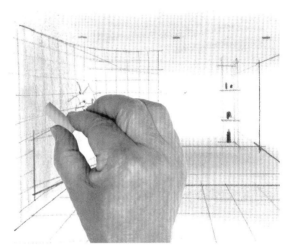

㉑ Color the wall of glass blocks with a light blue pastel

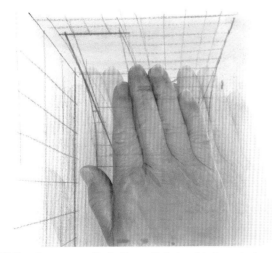

㉒ Turn the paper vertically (the wall of glass blocks on top), and then smooth out the pastel to create graduated shading

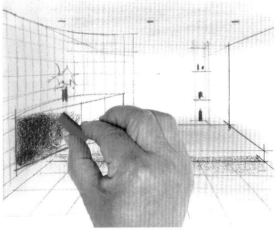

㉓ Turn the paper back and then color the storage unit

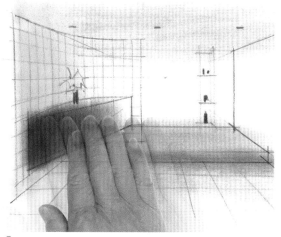

㉔ Smooth out with your fingertips

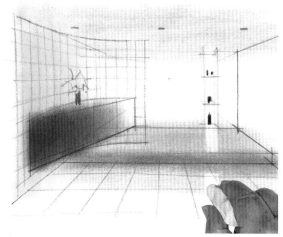

㉕ Render the reflection of the shelving on the floor

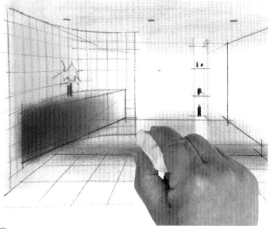

㉖ Using a kneaded eraser to brighten the right side of the glass block wall

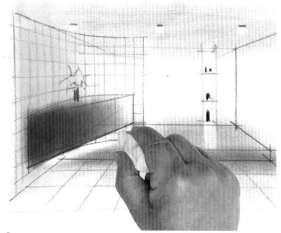

㉗ Render indirect lighting under the storage unit using a kneaded eraser

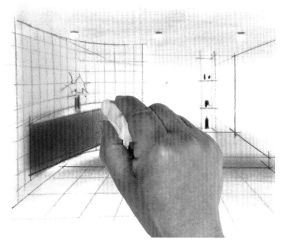

㉘ Brighten top surface of the storage unit with a kneaded eraser

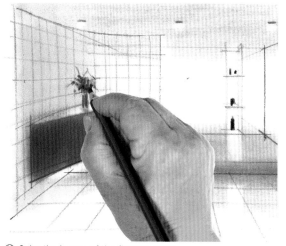

㉙ Color the leaves of the flowers green

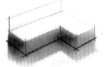

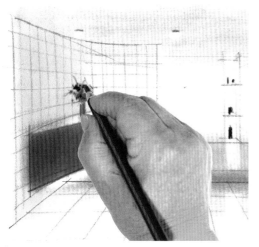

㉚ Color the red flowers next

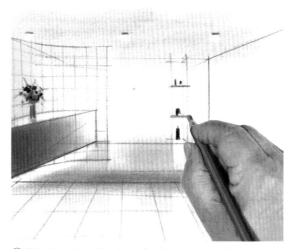

㉛ Color the edge of each shelf with a green pencil

㉜ Use white-out to render: Light from the pot-lights, light shining down on the flowers, and indirect light under the storage unit

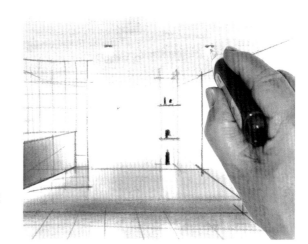

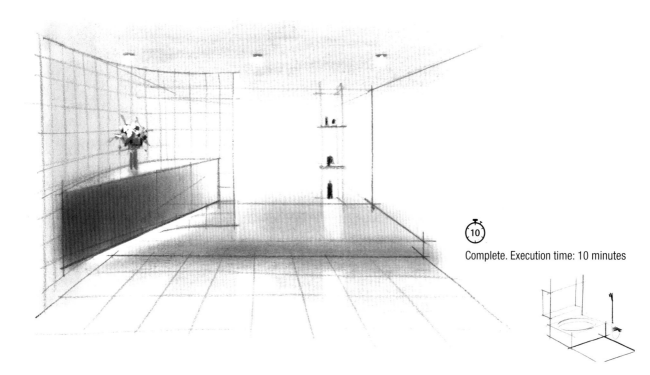

Complete. Execution time: 10 minutes

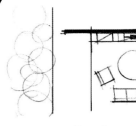
⏱ ⑧ [8 Minute Sketch]
Imagine Drinking a Beer while Admiring the Bamboo

Floor plan

This living room has large windows and an arched ceiling. Drawn in one-point perspective. Bamboo can be viewed through the window on the left. The layout of the shelves purposefully creates a certain asymmetry.

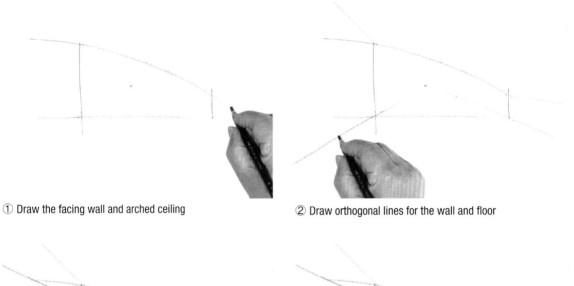

① Draw the facing wall and arched ceiling

② Draw orthogonal lines for the wall and floor

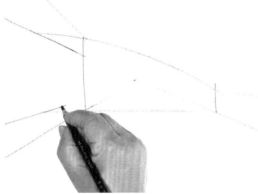

③ Draw some eaves and a veranda

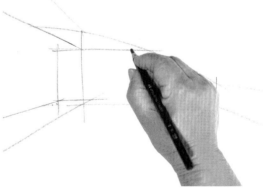

④ Draw the wall line

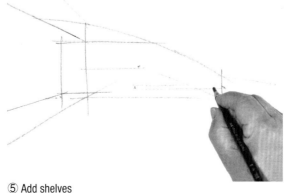

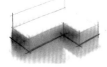

⑤ Add shelves

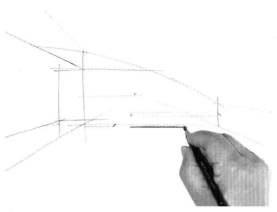

⑥ Layout some storage furniture

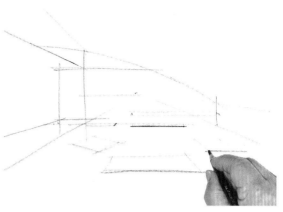

⑦ Layout a sofa

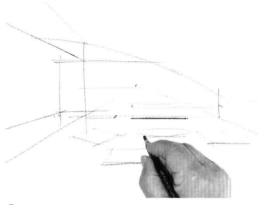

⑧ Layout a coffee table

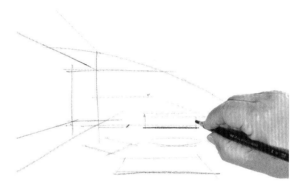

⑨ Draw the storage portion of the TV stand

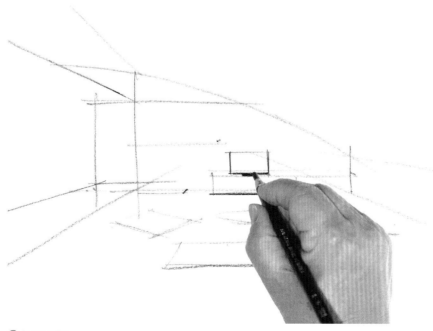

⑩ Draw a TV

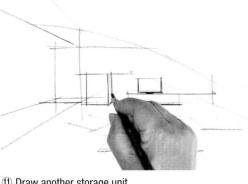

⑪ Draw another storage unit

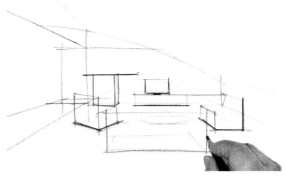

⑫ While varying lineweight, draw a three-dimensional sofa

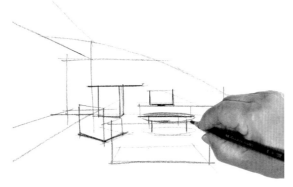

⑬ Add height to the coffee table

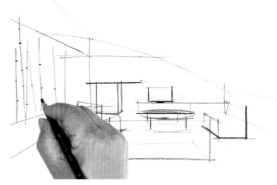

⑭ Draw simplified bamboo

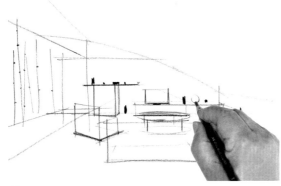

⑮ Draw décor articles

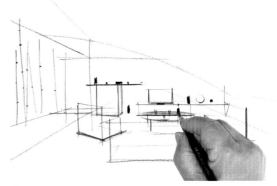

⑯ Draw dishes

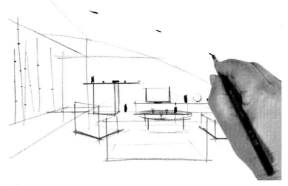

⑰ While gauging overall balance, draw downlights on the ceiling

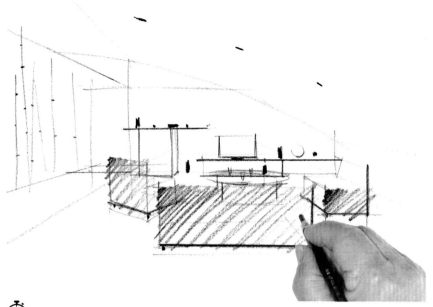

⏱ **(4)** ⑱ Add shade on the sofa to complete (approx. 4 min.)

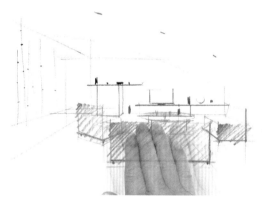

⑲ Apply and smooth out some white pastel to create a base for coloring

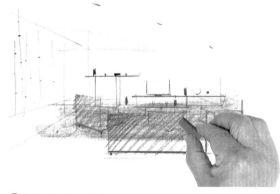

⑳ Color the floor dark gray

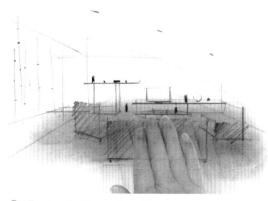

㉑ Smooth out with your fingertips

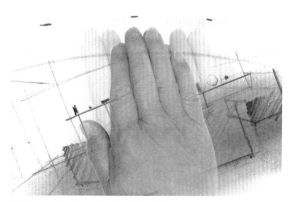

㉒ Also, color the arched ceiling dark gray and smooth it out

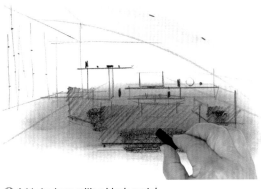

㉓ Add shadows with a black pastel

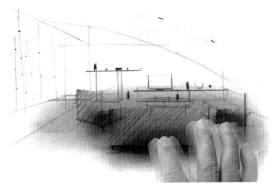

㉔ Smooth with fingertips

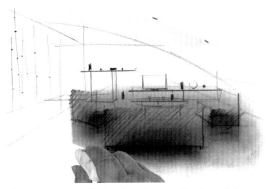

㉕ Erase the pastel below the window with a kneaded eraser

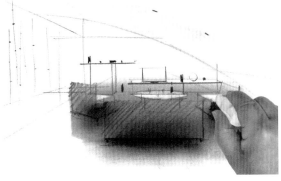

㉖ With a kneaded eraser brighten the seat of the sofa and the surface of the coffee table

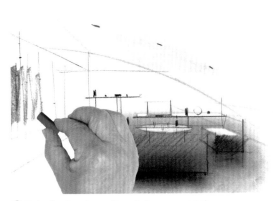

㉗ Color the bamboo with a dark green pastel

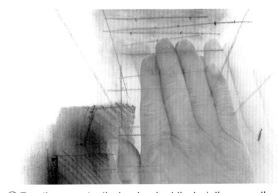

㉘ Turn the paper (so the bamboo is at the top), then smooth out the pastel

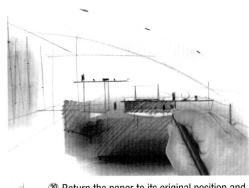

㉙ Return the paper to its original position and color the storage unit with a red color pencil

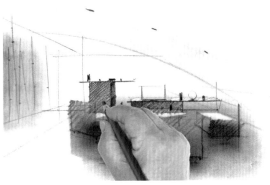

㉚ Change the color to navy blue and color another storage unit

㉜ Add light in the pot-lights using white-out

㉛ Emphasize the bamboo using a dark green color pencil

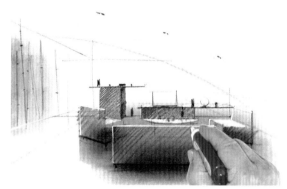

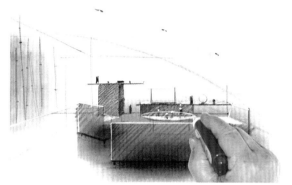

㉝ Outline the sofa's backrest, etc. Trace with a white-out

㉞ Adjust the coffee table and beer's froth using a white-out to complete

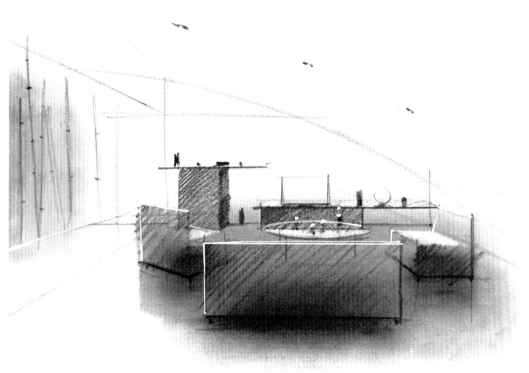

 Execution time: 8 minutes

⏱️ [10 Minute Sketch] Open Concept Spacious Living, Dining, and Kitchen Area

Floor plan

This section includes a living, dining, and kitchen space that is approximately 432 ft². Use one-point perspective to draw. The kitchen has a breakfast bar. A round dining set is placed in the garden so that you can enjoy a meal under in the shade. In order to clearly convey our ideas, we must raise the vanishing point. That way the furniture will not overlap.

① Draw the facing wall

② Draw orthogonal lines for the wall and floor

③ Add a window and door

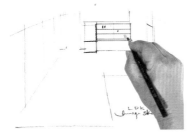

④ Draw a fridge and china cabinet

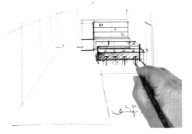

⑤ While adding shade, draw a kitchen counter and breakfast bar

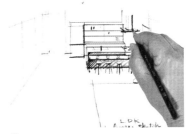

⑥ Draw a range hood

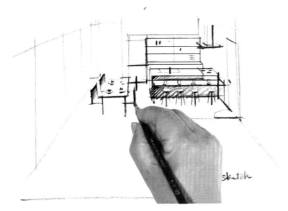

⑦ Draw a dining table set (including dishes)

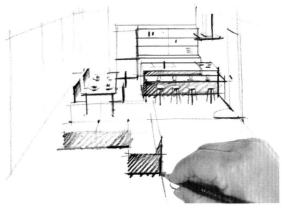

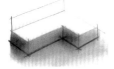

⑧ Draw a sofa

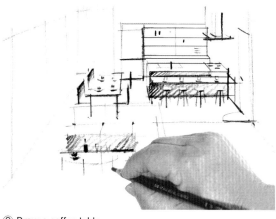

⑨ Draw a coffee table

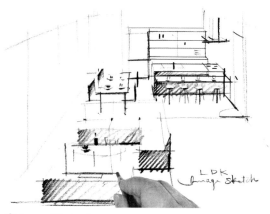

⑩ Draw a TV stand

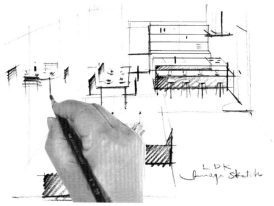

⑪ Draw a round table in the garden

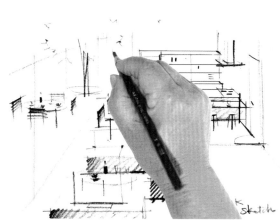

⑫ Draw a tree to complete

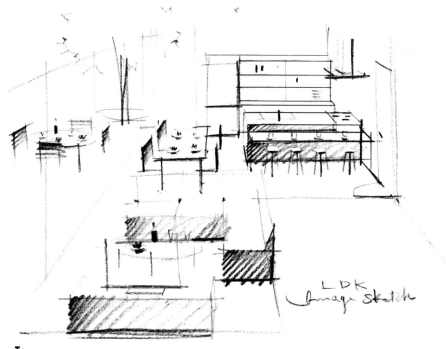

⑬ Execution time: 6 minutes

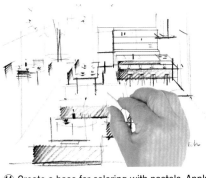

⑭ Create a base for coloring with pastels. Apply white pastel over everything

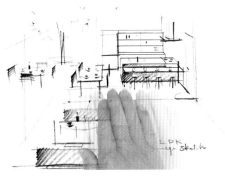

⑮ Smooth out the floor in its entirety. Since this is a relatively large area, use the tips of your fingers and move them horizontally using your entire arm

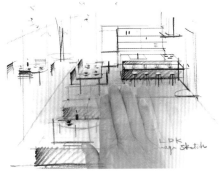

⑯ Apply the floor color (brown) pastel and then smooth it out with your fingertips

⑰ After adding shadows with black pastel, smooth them out

⑱ With a kneaded eraser, erase the pastel applied on the floor where there should be a reflection from the sliding window

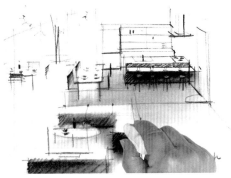

⑲ With a kneaded eraser, brighten the kitchen countertop, table surface, and seat of the sofa

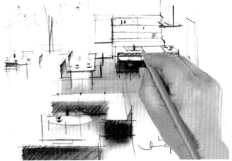

⑳ Use a blue color pencil to color the glass in the china cabinet and the kitchen sink

㉑ Use a navy blue color pencil to finish the sofa

㉒ Color the dishes on the table with a red color pencil

㉓ Color the edges of the coffee table with a green color pencil

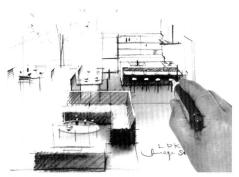

㉔ Brighten-up areas that need it with white-out to complete

⑩ Execution time: 10 minutes (Note: Coloring trees just blurs the drawing so they are left without color on purpose)

⑤ [5 Minute Sketch] A Bedroom with a Counter

This section is of a bedroom that is approximately 236 ft². Use two-point perspective. A low counter, matching the height of the sofa, is installed along the width of the room to provide a space to relax and enjoy some wine.

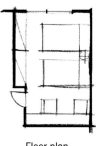

Floor plan

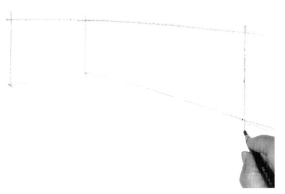

① Draw a wall

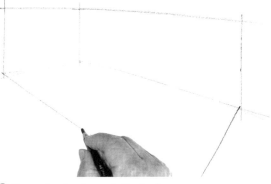

② Draw a line for storage in the front

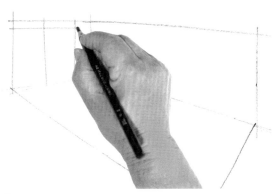

③ Draw a sliding window

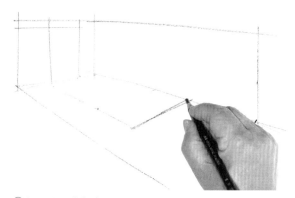

④ Layout each bed

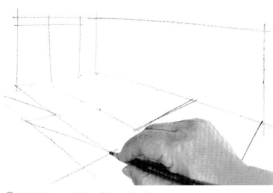

⑤ Mark the position of the closet

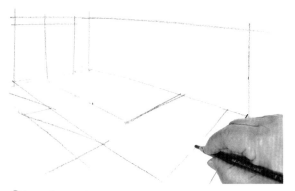

⑥ Layout a counter

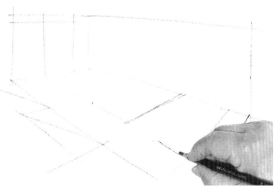

⑦ Layout two chairs

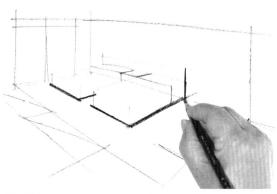

⑧ Add height to the bed (varying lineweight)

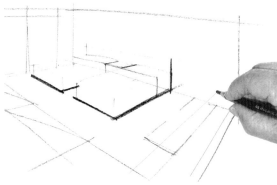

⑨ Draw a counter in the foreground

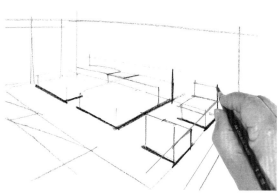

⑩ Add height to the chair (varying lineweight)

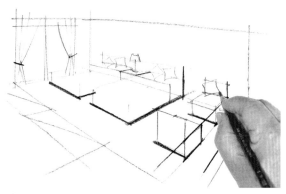

⑪ Add some cushions on the bed and chair. Then add a lamp

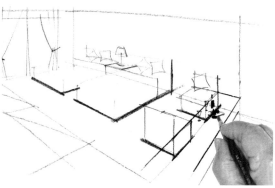

⑫ Draw dishes on the counter

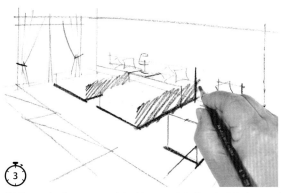

⑬ Draw shadows on each bed to complete the sketch. Approx. 3 min.

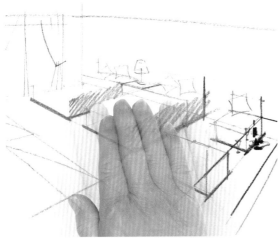

⑭ Create a base for coloring with pastels. Apply white pastel over the entire area and smooth it out

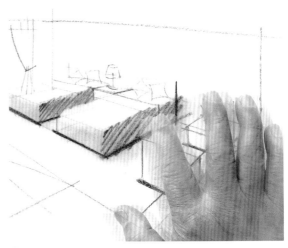

⑮ Rubbing the shadows drawn with a dermatgraph pencil creates softer shadows

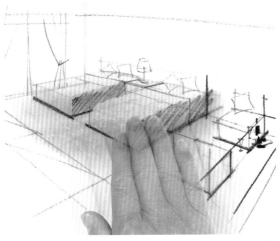

⑯ Apply brown pastel for the floor, and then smooth it out with your fingertips

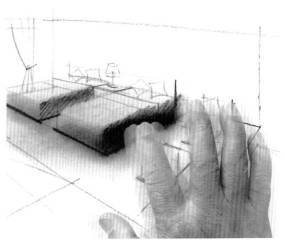

⑰ Add shadows with black pastel and smooth them out

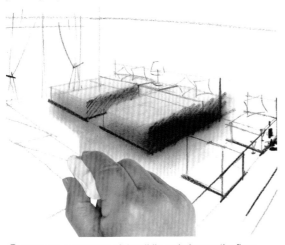

⑱ Render the reflection of the sliding window on the floor

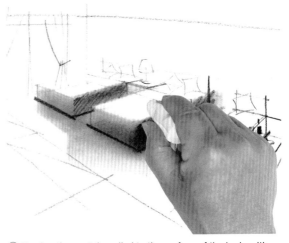

⑲ Erasing the pastel applied to the surface of the beds with a kneaded eraser brings out the three-dimensional feel of the beds

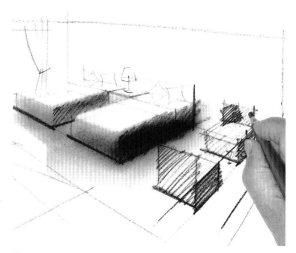

⑳ Use a navy blue color pencil for the sofa

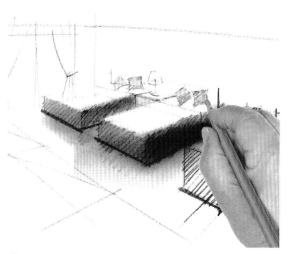

㉑ Use a brown color pencil for the cushions and red and yellow for the dishes on the counter

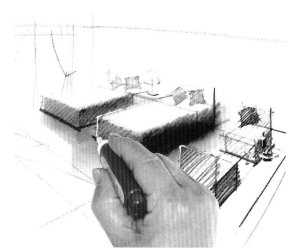

㉒ Touch up areas that need brightening with white-out to complete

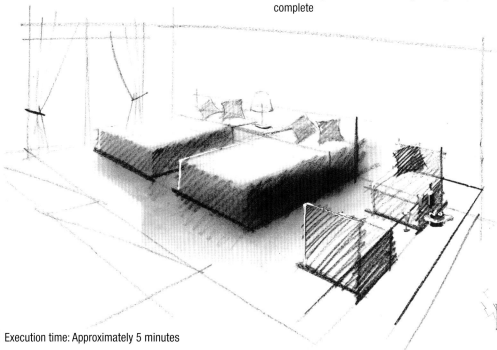

🕐⑤ Execution time: Approximately 5 minutes

⑦ [7 Minute Sketch]
A Space for Hosting Senior Leisure Time

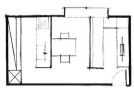

Floor plan

This living, dining, and kitchen area is approximately 314 ft². The concept of this floor plan is a space where a married couple can happily spend their leisure time. The sofa and TV stand are designed as a single piece. By suggesting an image of how someone might spend their time in a space, and not just proposing furniture design ideas, a design sketch becomes a great decision-making aid in regards to gaining approval from a client for proposed interior design work.

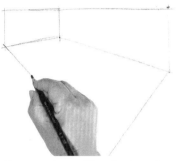

① Draw orthogonal lines for the wall and floor

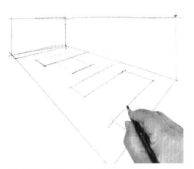

② While looking at the floor plan, layout the appliances and furniture

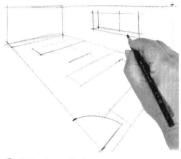

③ Add a bay window

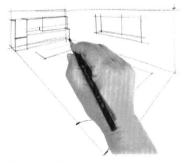

④ Draw a fridge and china cabinet

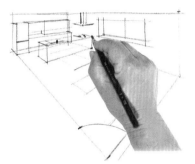

⑤ Draw a kitchen counter

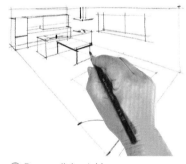

⑥ Draw a dining table

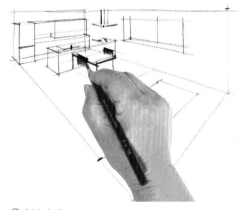

⑦ Add chairs

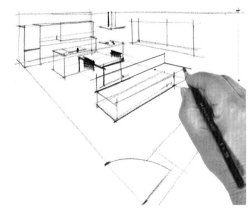

⑧ Draw a sofa

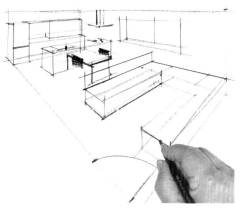

⑨ Draw a TV stand

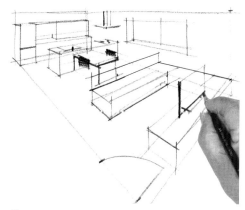

⑩ Draw a TV

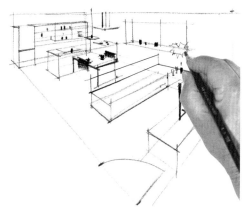

⑪ Add some dinnerware, dishes, and a potted plant

⑫ Since the bay is located on the right side, you should draw shadows on the left side of your furniture

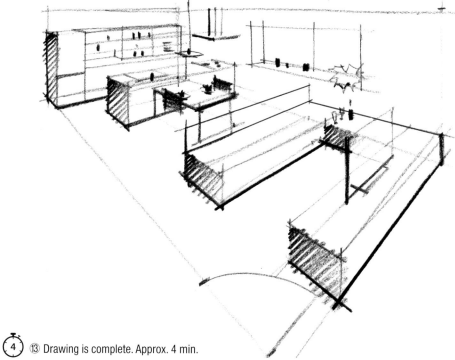

 ⑬ Drawing is complete. Approx. 4 min.

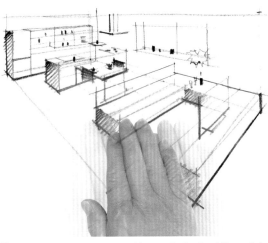

⑭ Create a base for coloring with pastels. Apply white pastel over the designated area and smooth it out

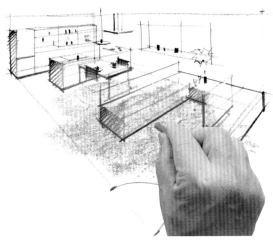

⑮ Color a floor with brown pastel

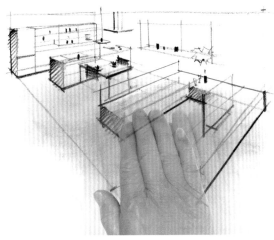

⑯ Smooth the entire floor area

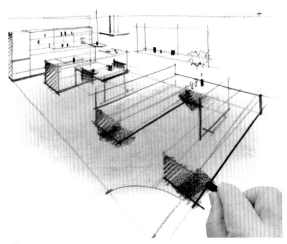

⑰ Add shadows with black pastel

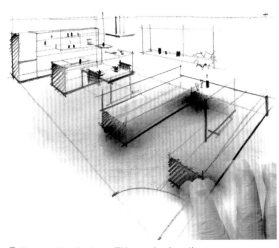

⑱ Smooth the shadows. This emphasizes them

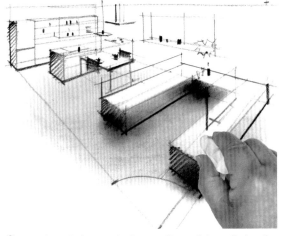

⑲ Use a kneaded eraser to clean up the pastels applied on the surface of the furniture

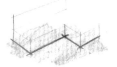

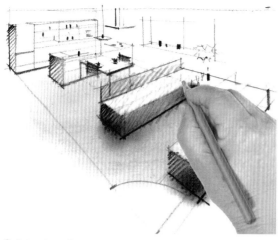

⑳ Color the sofa with a brown color pencil using uniformly angled strokes (about 45-degree)

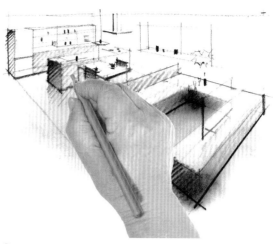

㉑ Color the china cabinet and kitchen counter with the same angled pencil strokes as the sofa

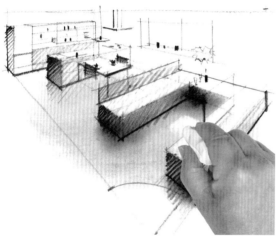

㉒ Use a kneaded eraser to render the reflections of the bay window on the floor

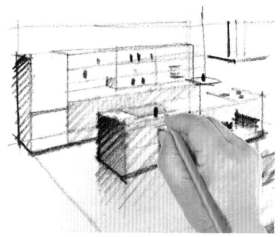

㉓ Color the glass of the china cabinet and the kitchen sink (using approx. 45-degree angled strokes)

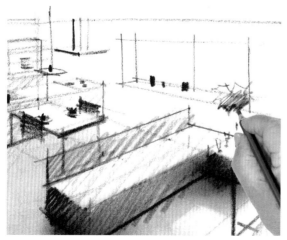

㉔ Color the potted plant using color pencils (approx. 45-degree angled strokes)

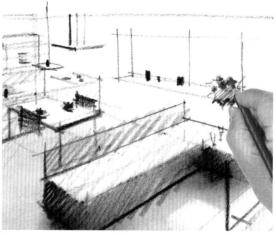

㉕ Color the flowers using color pencils

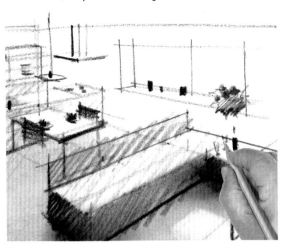

㉖ Color the beer in each glass using color pencils

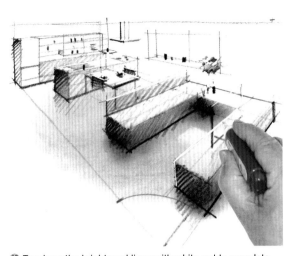

㉗ Touch up the brightened lines with white-out to complete

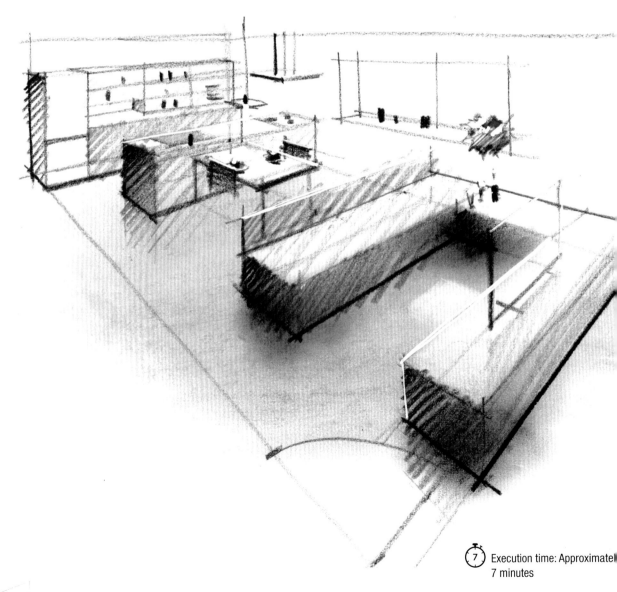

Execution time: Approximate 7 minutes

⑤ [5 Minute Sketch] A House with an Ocean View

This is a plan for a house right by the ocean. Use one-point perspective to draw. The design concept is intended to be one where a married couple can just spend some leisure time hanging around the house. This floor plan includes ample space and provides a view of the ocean throughout the house—a matter of course on the outside deck. No matter where you are in a house, whether relaxing in the living room, cooking in the kitchen, or dining at the table, you will always have an ocean view.

Floor plan

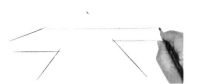

① Roughly draw a floor, while constantly referencing the floor plan

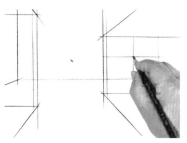

② Draw a window once the wall is formed

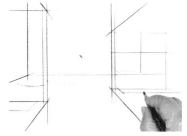

③ Layout a table on the deck, an interior sofa, and a kitchen counter

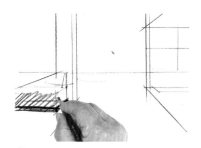

④ Form a three-dimensional sofa

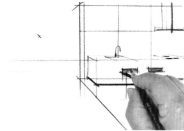

⑤ Draw a kitchen counter and a dining table set

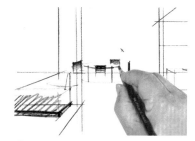

⑥ Draw a table and chairs on the deck

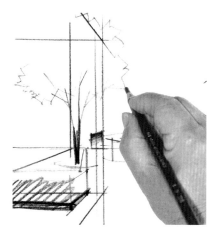

⑦ Draw a tree

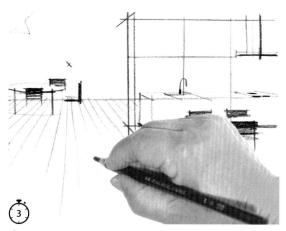

⑧ Quickly draw out the decking. Complete (approx. 3 min.)

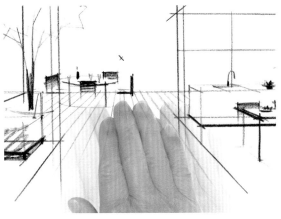

⑨ Using white pastel to prepare to color

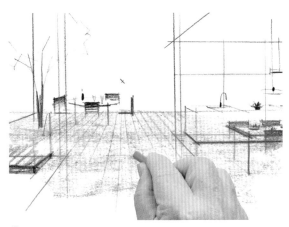

⑩ Color the deck with pastel

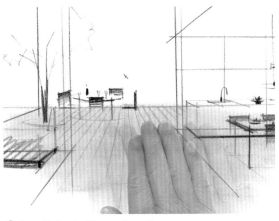

⑪ Smooth it out with your fingertips

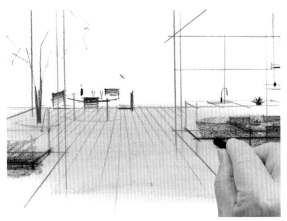

⑫ Add shadows on the sofa and the kitchen counter with black pastel

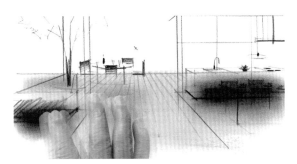

⑬ Evenly smooth out the shadows with your fingertips

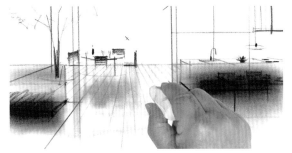

⑭ Erase excess pastel—except the reflection of the table set on the deck—using a kneaded eraser

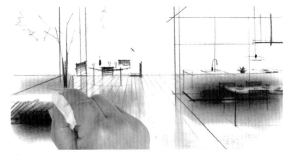

⑮ Brighten the kitchen counter-top, the surface of the table, and the seat of the sofa with a kneaded eraser

Chapter 5 Speedsketch Presentation

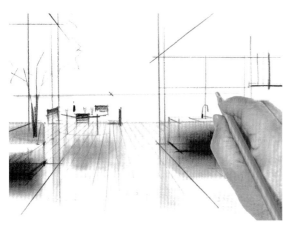

⑯ Add a relatively thin line representing the ocean in one go. Use a color pencil. A ruler can be used as well

⑰ Add colors to the dishes, etc.

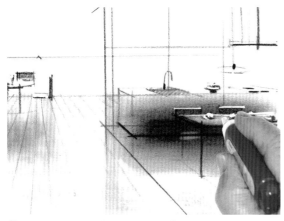

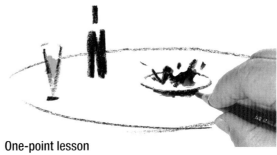

⑱ Touch-up with a white-out to complete

One-point lesson

Use alphabet letters "I" and "M" to render a beer bottle. Draw thick and dark. Use the yellow color pencil for the beer and white-out for its froth. For the dishes lightly draw a plate (oval shape) first. Then, add shadows under the plate. Draw food on the plate dark, thick, and strong, and then color it red (using a color pencil). Touch-up with a white-out to accentuate.

  The key point here is simplicity. Execution time: Approximately 5 minutes

⑤ [5 Minute Sketch] A House with a Symbolic Tree

A tree, symbolizing this house, is seen from a large sliding window. Though the tree is the key point here, priority should be given to drawing the living room space. Only after drawing the interior space do we begin to draw the tree. The methods for simplifying and coloring the tree will be introduced on P. 142. Please refer to that section and compare those steps to the ones in this section.

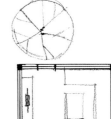

Floor plan

① Draw the facing wall

② Draw orthogonal lines for the wall and floor

③ Add lines for the window

④ Layout a TV stand

⑤ Draw the sofa while gauging overall balance

⑥ Layout a coffee table

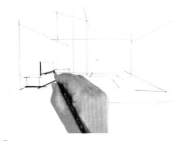

⑦ Draw a TV stand with varying lineweights

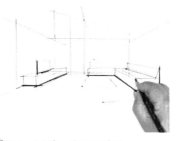

⑧ Draw a sofa using varying lineweights

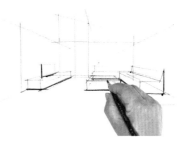

⑨ Draw a coffee table

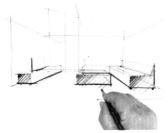

⑩ Draw shadows on the furniture

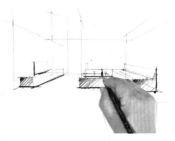

⑪ Draw dishes on the table

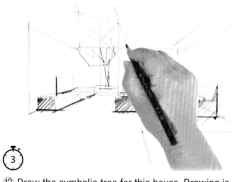

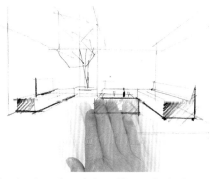

⑫ Draw the symbolic tree for this house. Drawing is complete. Approx. 3 min.

⑬ Create a base for coloring with pastels. Apply white pastel and smooth it out

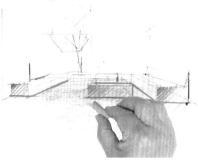

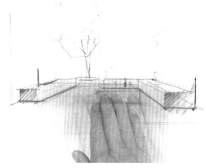

⑭ Color the floor with dark gray

⑮ Smooth out the floor using your fingertips

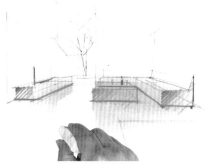

⑯ Render reflections from the window using a kneaded eraser

⑰ Add brightness to the seat of the sofa, etc. with a kneaded eraser

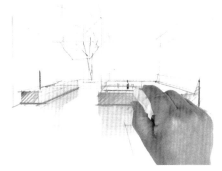

⑱ Add brightness to the coffee table

⑲ Color the shadow using a black pastel

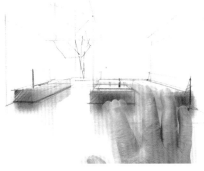

⑳ Smooth the shadows with your fingertips

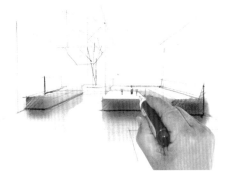

㉑ Using a white-out to draw the beer froth, etc.

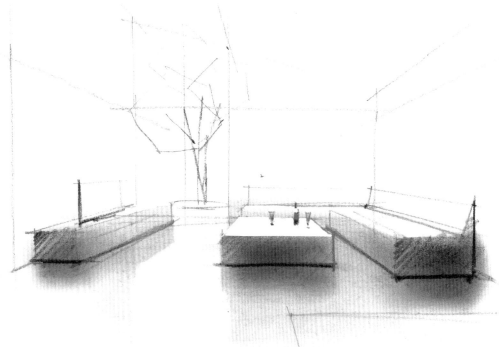

🕔 Complete. Execution time: Approximately 5 minutes

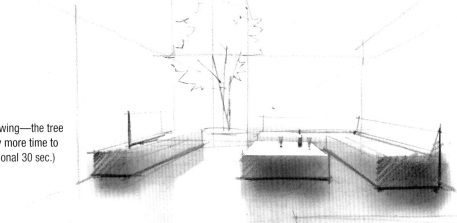

Sample drawing—the tree
took slightly more time to
draw (additional 30 sec.)

Chapter 5 Speedsketch Presentation

Chapter 6

Items that Expand
Interior Design Sketches

In this chapter methods for drawing human figures, pets, plants, etc., that help to amplify the sense of "lifestyle" found within interior architectural spaces are detailed. By adding the seasonal expressions of plants an interior design sketch becomes a lot more attractive.

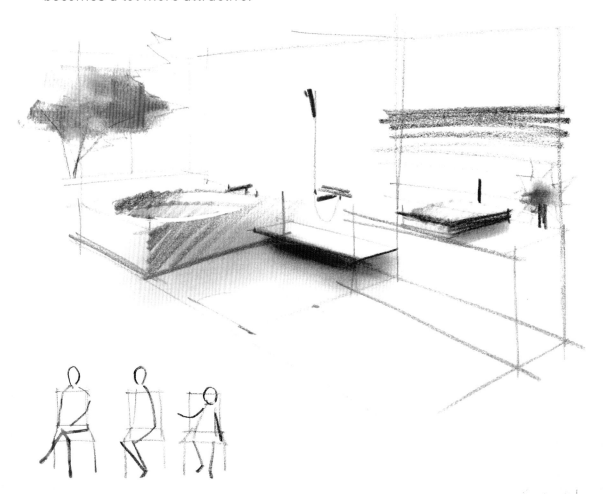

Drawing Human Figures 1

Even without drawing human figures, interior design sketches can adequately convey the overall image of a space. In this section we will try to draw human figures in order to expand the image of our designed space. For example, it is perhaps easier to convey the pleasant atmosphere associated with conversations around a dinner table, or the relaxed feel created by having close friends over, etc., by adding human figures. However, in speedsketching, human figures are rendered in a very simple manner by excluding detailed facial expressions, etc.

A scene where friends have come over and everyone is having a pleasant time in the living, dining, and kitchen space (3 min.)

Having a conversation while enjoying a glass of wine

From the left, a male, a female, and a child

A person relaxes at a table

Friendly conversation

A child and parent

A couple relaxing on a sofa

Family time on the sofa

Family mealtime at a table

A family enjoying their meal

A party scene with close friends (3 min.)

Let's try to add a person to an interior design drawing of a living, dining, and kitchen space.

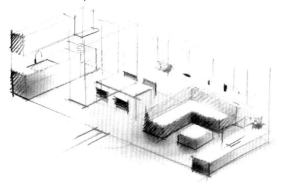

① Draw a living, dining, and kitchen space that is approx. 314 ft² (approx. 6 min.)

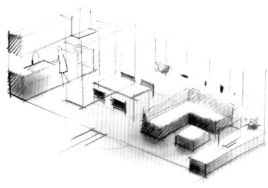

② Draw a woman in front of the kitchen counter (additional 10 sec.)

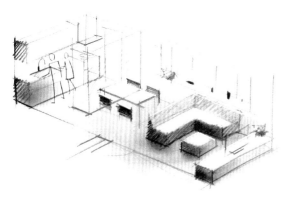

③ Draw a man next to the woman (additional 10 sec.)

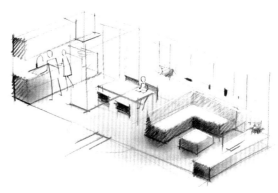

④ Draw a child at a dining table. Watch for overall balance (additional 10 sec.)

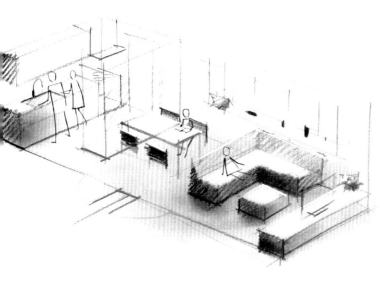

⑤ Draw a child on the sofa (additional 10 sec.). Adding people deepens the impression of an interior design drawing (total approx. 7 min.)

A family talking in their dining and kitchen space

A family talking in their living room

Drawing Human Figures 2

Let's practice drawing a woman, man, and child. Since this is speedsketching, simplify as much as you can. Omit hair, facial expressions, etc. Draw clothing by simplifying. Let's practice so that you can finish your drawings in about 10 seconds. The position of the arms and the way they are bent describe the differences in each person's movement.

■ **Draw a woman**

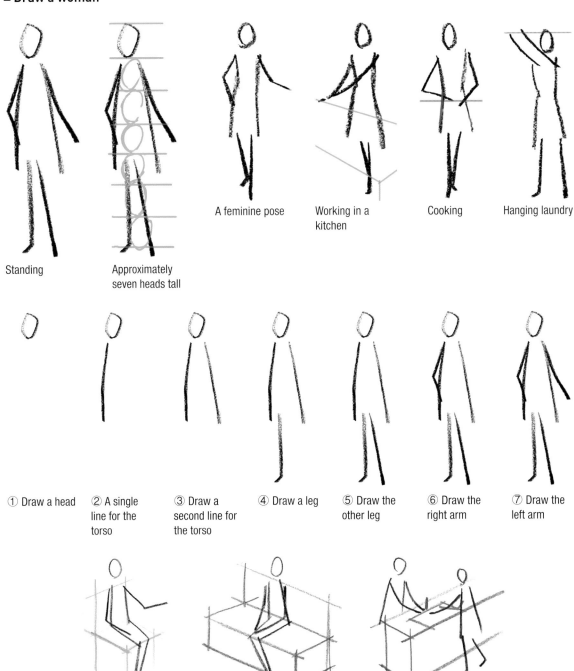

A feminine pose

Working in a kitchen

Cooking

Hanging laundry

Standing

Approximately seven heads tall

① Draw a head ② A single line for the torso ③ Draw a second line for the torso ④ Draw a leg ⑤ Draw the other leg ⑥ Draw the right arm ⑦ Draw the left arm

Sitting in a chair

Sitting on a sofa

Working in a kitchen

■ Drawing a man

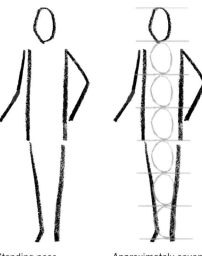

Standing pose

Approximately seven heads tall

Reaching up to grasp an object

■ Drawing a child

A childlike pose

Depending on the child's age this will change, but generally children are four heads tall

A man and a wheelchair. Use a color pencil for the wheelchair

A girl talking to someone

A childlike pose

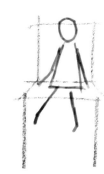

A girl sitting in a chair

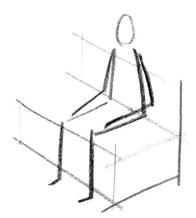

A man sitting on a sofa

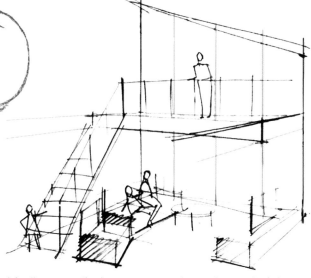

A family conversation in an open-concept space (approx. 3 min.)

Drawing a Pet

A pet drawn in an interior design sketch can play a very important role in adding "feel". For instance, the calm and relaxed feeling associated with drawing a cat laying on a sofa will definitely appeal to cat lovers. This book deals with "cats" and "dogs". Let's draw simplified figures in about 10 seconds, in a similar manner to drawing human figures.

■ Draw a cat

Drawing cats sleeping, instead of standing, brings out the cat's innate character

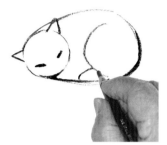

Sleeping cat (approx. 10 sec.)

A cat sleeping comfortably on a sofa (total approx. 30 sec.)

① Draw an oval (the torso)

② Draw a circle (the head)

③ Draw another circle (the femur) slightly bigger than the head

④ Add ears at an angle

⑤ Draw feet

⑥ Draw eyes to complete

■ Draw a kitten

A sleeping pose for kitten's can be completed with just an oval and two circles.

① A kitten's sleeping pose

② Balance while aiming for an overall length of two heads

■ Drawing a dog

There are various breeds of dog of course, but here we choose to draw the easier ones.

A child and a dog playing (approx. 40 sec.)

A sitting dog (approx. 20 sec.)

① Draw an oval (the torso)

② Draw a line for the neckline

③ Draw another line for the neckline

④ Draw the contour of the face

⑤ Draw the head

⑥ Draw a circle for the femur

⑦ Draw the feet

⑧ Draw the ear

⑨ Draw the eye and nose to complete

■ Draw a puppy

Just watching a puppy sleeping makes most people feel better, even if they are not dog lovers.

① A puppy sleeping

② Try for a balance that is two heads long

Drawing a Tree

By including nature in an interior design drawing, we can create a certain depth of space and a comfortable atmosphere. The shape of a tree itself is a manifestation of nature, so every tree has a different shape. This book provides clues for simplifying the tree shape and demonstrates how to create a sense of season through coloring.

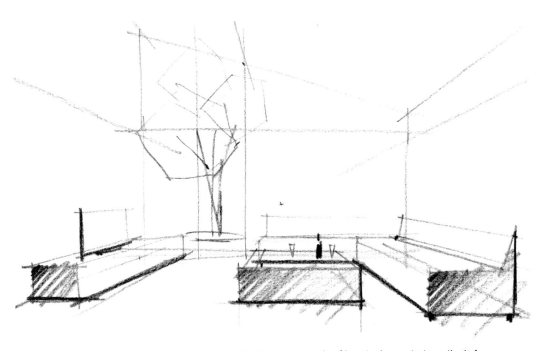

This section uses "A house with a symbolic tree" on P. 132 as an example of how to demonstrate methods for simplifying and coloring

① Draw an oval to determine the position of the tree's roots. Next, draw a line upward

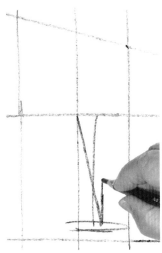

② Draw splits in the trunk as freely as you can

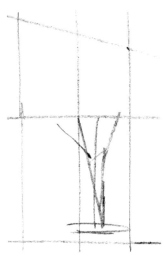

③ Draw trunk extensions and branches

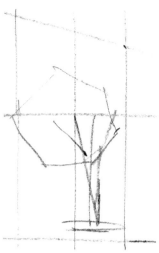

④ In this example, we will draw a tree canopy that is divided into three clumps. Draw the largest first

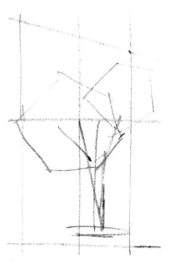

⑤ Next, draw the slightly smaller one

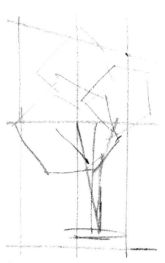

⑥ Lastly, draw the smallest clump in order to complete our sketch (approx. 20 sec.)

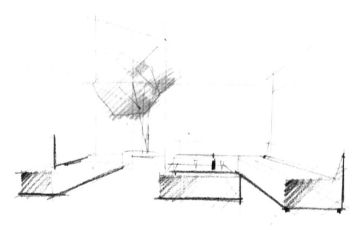

An example of coloring with pencils. Add depth by rendering the tree canopy in three sections with varying amounts of shading (colored with pencils 30 sec.)

Color pencil: Dark green

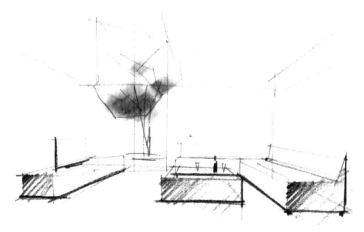

An example of coloring with pastels. Directly apply pastel to the paper and rub it in with your fingertips to achieve a blurred finish (colored with pastels 30 sec.)

Pastel: Dark green

Let's take a little more time to add expressions to the tree canopy. This is speedsketching though, so try to finish your drawing in under 30 seconds. It may be difficult to draw a tree canopy, but with repetition you will become more and more proficient at generating your own tree shapes.

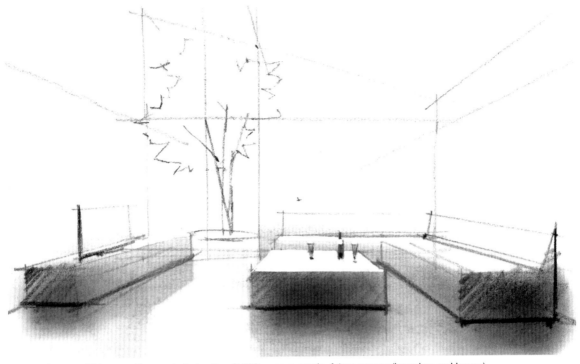

This section uses "A house with a symbolic tree" on P. 132 as an example. A tree canopy (branches and leaves)

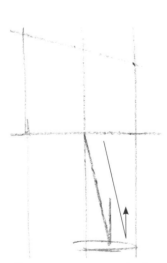

① Draw an oval to determine the position of the tree root. Begin to draw with the trunk

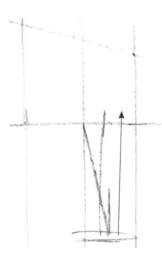

② Draw another trunk

③ Add branches and trunk extensions

④ Begin to draw a tree canopy

⑤ Draw the shape of the tree canopy while leaving some to the imagination

⑥ Draw using imperfect lines, because if the shape is too perfect the overall look becomes unnatural

⑦ After drawing the tree canopy with varying lineweights, it is complete (approx. 30 sec.)

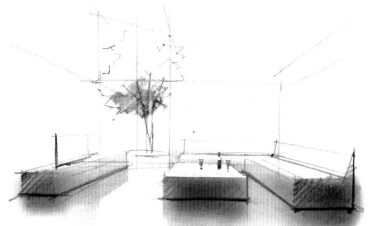
An example of coloring with pencils. Create the canopy with shading. The key point is to avoid filling in the whole canopy (colored with pencils 20 sec.)

Color pencil: Dark green

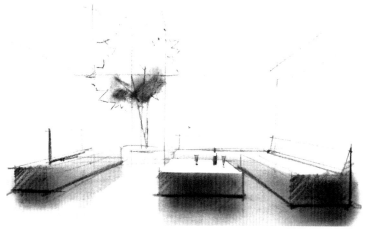
Directly apply pastel on the paper and rub it with your fingertips to achieve a blurred finish. A key point here is to avoid filling in the entire canopy (colored with pastels 20 sec.)

Pastel: Dark green

Creating Seasons by Adding Color to Trees

Since cherry trees bloom in spring they are strongly associated with images of spring. However, cherry trees can be enjoyed throughout the year. The colors and shapes of the tree canopy vary each season and it is interesting to use different coloring mediums in order to distinctly render each season.

[Color pencils]
White, red, yellow, and dark green. These four colors are used to create the four seasons.

■ **Create the four seasons with color pencils**

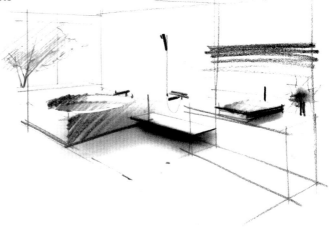

① A cherry tree peeking out from a bay window in a bathroom can intimate one of the four seasons. In "winter" the leaves have fallen and the branches are exposed so there is essentially no coloring

② For the cherry tree in "spring", you can add color with a red pencil in a pale, thin, and gentle manner. Then, lay over a white color pencil to create pink cherry blossoms

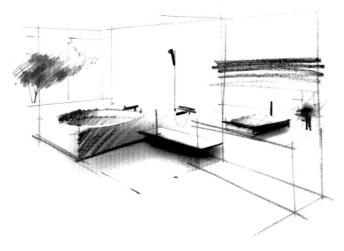

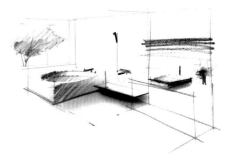

③ Rendering "summer" is simple. Just add color with a dark green pencil while adjusting the strength of your pencil strokes

④ Autumn leaves in the "fall" are the highlight of the four seasons. Put yellow on first, then adjust with red to finish up

[Pastels]
White, red, yellow, and dark green. These four colors are used to create the four seasons.

■ Creating the four seasons with color pastels

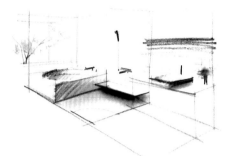

① By coloring a tree that is peeking up through a bay window in a bathroom, you can create the image of one of the four seasons. "Spring" is associated with cherry trees. Lay down some white pastel first. Then, apply a little bit of red (minimal) and subtly blend it in to create the blossoms

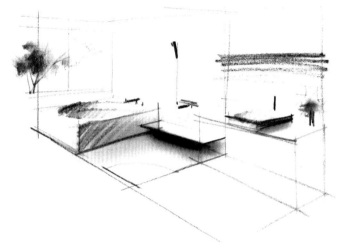

② Creating "summer" is relatively easy with a dark green pastel. The type of tree doesn't really matter when rendering summer. Color the bottom 1/3 of the tree canopy (do not color too strongly)

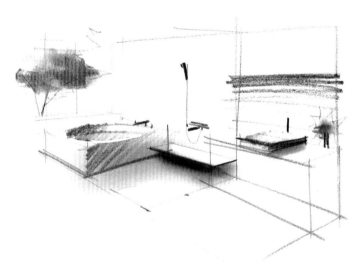

③ Use yellow and red pastels to create "fall". The tree type for fall is definitely the maple. Use yellow first and lay down thick and dense red.

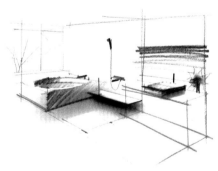

④ No coloring is necessary when rendering "winter". You just need bare branches.

Let's Draw Seasonal Sense into Each Section

This is the method for creating interior design sketches that add seasonal appeal. Just by adding a tree, your interior design sketch will become more attractive. It is a huge asset to be able to enjoy nature in your everyday life. Studying techniques in rendering appliances and furniture is important, I also recommend that you do your best to properly render the trees in this book.

At the end of the hall, a cherry tree is seen. Colored with pastels (total 8 min.)

A cherry tree in the garden is seen from a large window by the staircase (total 10 min.)

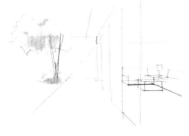

There is a tree by the deck. Enjoy sunlight filtering down through its branches and also its shade. Use white-out for the sunlight (total 5 min.)

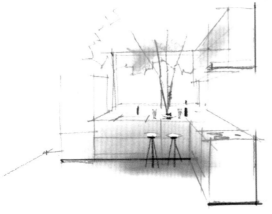

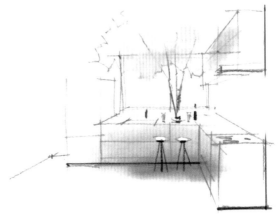

The next house's cherry tree is seen through a window in the kitchen. The examples noted above are given the seasonal feel of "summer" or "spring". On the right, we see pink cherry blossoms that harken to spring

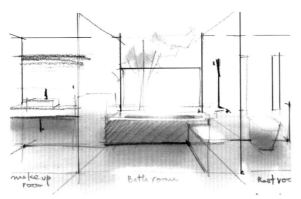

From a bathroom window, a tree is seen. Sunlight filtering down through the tree would make anyone comfortable (total 10min.)

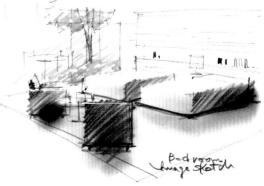

Outside of the bedroom we find abundant green plants. Add color with pencils while matching the angles on the bedroom wall. If you try you just might feel the sunlight and wind outside (total approx. 8 min.)

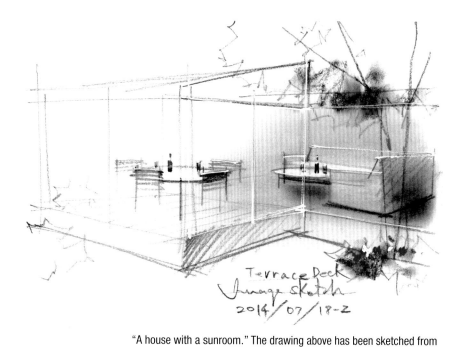

Terrace Deck
Image sketch
2014/07/18-2

"A house with a sunroom." The drawing above has been sketched from the vantage point of the garden. When the interior is sketched with too many details the pleasantness of the space decreases by about one half. Manual drawing has advantages in that it simplifies the details. Colored with pastels (total approx. 8 min.)

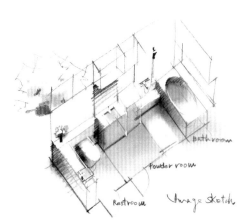

Living room
Image sketch

Autumn leaves can be seen from a living room window. The furniture is not colored so the autumn leaves are emphasized. As such, the interior design sketch looks much more impressive (total 8 min.)

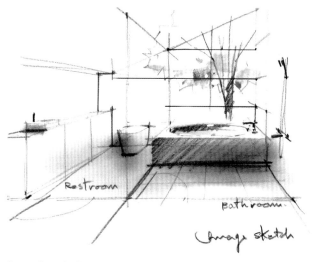

Restroom

Bathroom

Image sketch

From a large bathroom window, autumn leaves are seen. When proposing a bathroom space design, including nature generally increases the value of that space (total 8 min.)

Bathroom

Powder room

Restroom   Image sketch

Origami sketch. Use your isometric projection to draw this sketch. The attractiveness of a drawing varies greatly with the inclusion or exclusion of autumn leaves (total 10 min.)

Drawing Plants

Indoor plants make us to feel closer to nature. By comparing your drawing both with a plant and without one, you will see how much a plant adds richness and produces a sense of ease. An interior design sketch composed with furniture, appliances, and hardware alone tends to be used to "explain" the types of objects within a space. Let's draw plants while aiming to create warmth and feel within your drawing.

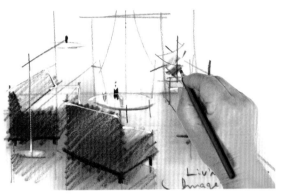

An indoor plant in a living room. Use color pencils

■ Drawing indoor plants

Though there are many different kinds of indoor plants, in this section we introduce just three kinds. Let's practice so that we become super proficient at drawing them casually in a small space (approx. 10 sec.)

① Draw a pot

② Draw a line

③ Draw rhythmically, in one stroke

④ Add a branch as an accent

⑤ Add a branch in the middle, on the right, as an accent

⑥ Draw a lager branch as an accent at the bottom left (drawing completed in 10 sec.)

An example of coloring with pencils. Color by making slight variations

An example of coloring with pastels. Color separately the areas you wish to blend and those to leave untouched

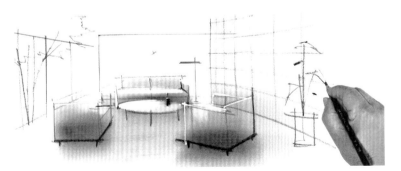

An example of an indoor plant that has been highlighted with large leaves

An indoor plant composed using triangular shapes (10 sec.)

An indoor plant composed using a circular shape (10 sec.)

An example of flowers displayed by a bay window in a dining/living area

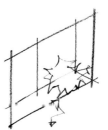

A flower (plant) by a bay window. Use your isometric projection to draw (20 sec.)

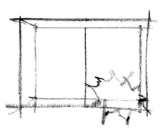

A flower (plant) by a bay window. Use one-point perspective to draw (20 sec.)

■ Draw flowers

Flower colors vary greatly. However, using just two colors, red and green, allows you to draw flowers speedily at a meeting.

① Outline flowers and leaves

② Color with green. At first, apply a pale layer

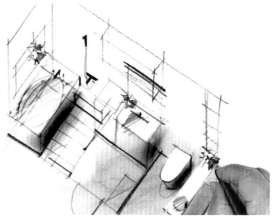

Add flowers to a bathroom design by drawing with isometric projection

③ Lay over some darker color

④ Draw flowers while changing their size

⑤ Adding white-out enriches your level expression (40 sec.)

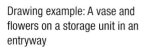

Drawing example: A vase and flowers on a storage unit in an entryway

Draw your vase and flowers dark and thick. The stems are thin (15 sec.)

① Draw your vase and flowers dark and thick. Make the overall shape of your flowers and their leaves natural (15 sec.)

② Color with pastels. Use white-out to add accents (total 30 sec.)

Appendix: Sketch Guide

This isometric perspective guideline consists of perpendicular and left-to-right 30-degree angled lines. Lay under your drawing to use.

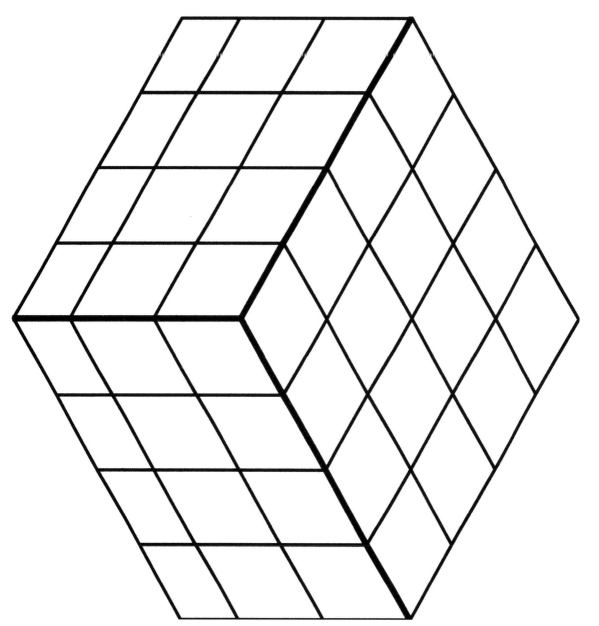

This isometric projection guideline is for spaces that are 360 cm (12 ft.) x 360 cm (12 ft.) x a ceiling height of 240cm (8 ft.) (approx. 157 ft² space)

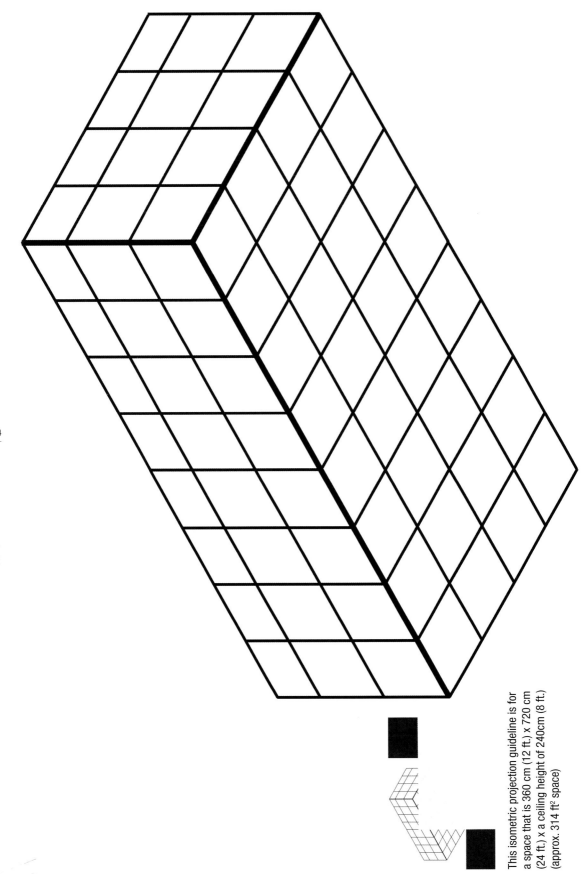

This isometric projection guideline is for a space that is 360 cm (12 ft.) x 720 cm (24 ft.) x a ceiling height of 240cm (8 ft.) (approx. 314 ft² space)

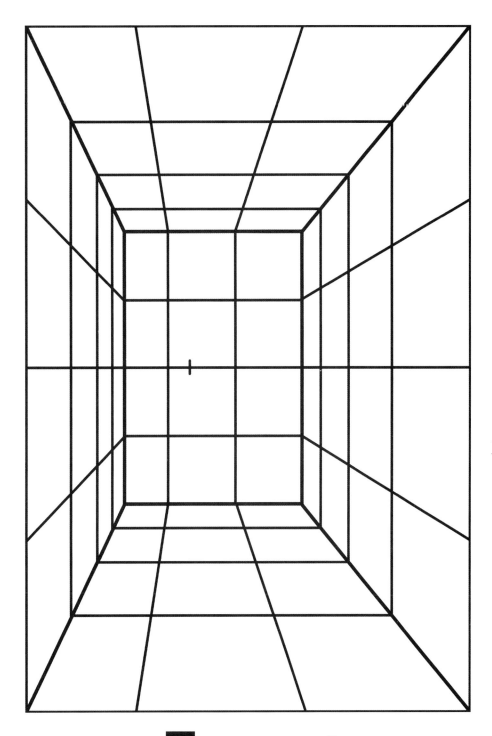

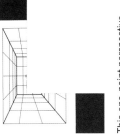

This one-point perspective
guideline is for a space that is
360 cm (12 ft.) x 360 cm (12 ft.)
x a ceiling height of 240cm (8 ft.)
(approx. 157 ft² space)

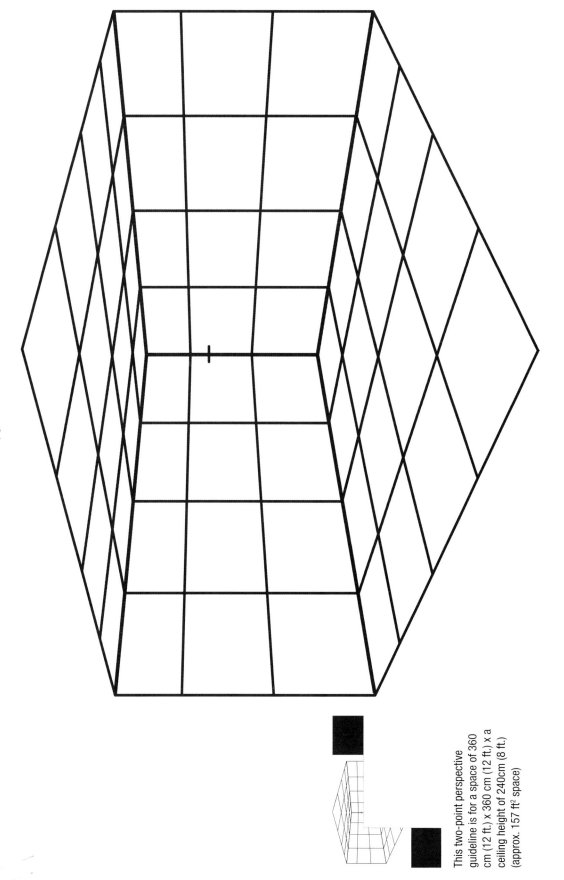

This two-point perspective guideline is for a space of 360 cm (12 ft.) x 360 cm (12 ft.) x a ceiling height of 240cm (8 ft.) (approx. 157 ft² space)

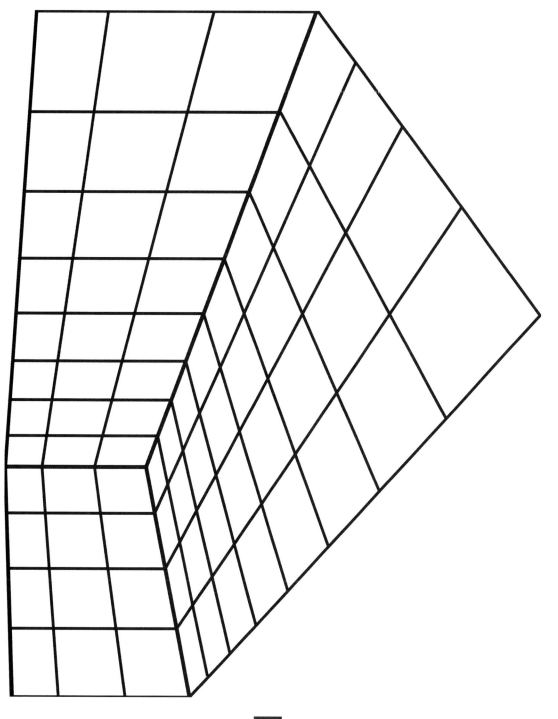

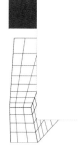

This two-point perspective guideline is for a space of 360 cm (12 ft.) x 720 cm (24 ft.) x a ceiling height of 240cm (8 ft.) (approx. 314 ft^2 space)

Afterword

Sketching Interiors was first published in 1995. *Sketching Interiors: A Step-By-Step Guide*, a revision of the first book, was published 10 years later in 2005. After another 10 years *Interior Design Presentations: Techniques for Quick, Professional Renderings for Interiors* was published. The objective of all of these books is to show you how to create "simple and easy to understand" interior design drawings that can be used at a meeting in the presence of a client. This philosophy has not changed in over 20 years, since the first book was published.

Due to remarkable advancements in digital technology, the method for giving housing design presentations has drastically changed. 20 years ago I would never have thought that digital gadgets would become so inexpensive and widely available as they are today. Digital technology can create such high quality perspective drawings that they can actually be mistaken for photographs. In addition, this technology allows us to create a proposal, with the accompanying estimates, during our meeting with a client. People who can't draw a lick are able to operate such technology. Furthermore, instead of using interior design drawings, a presentation can be given using an architectural model printed with a 3D printer. Under such circumstances you might ask, "why should we even draw designs now?" Of course in recent years people have sought more and more speed, so it is inevitable that we ask why time consuming manual sketches are even created when computers can do the work for you. Actually, I use a computer most of the time when I am performing desk-work. However, I do not use a computer at all when I am meeting with my clients. They might be slightly more time consuming to draw, but manually created memos and drawings suit me perfectly. I believe that experiencing the agility of manual drawing is quite important for a client when I give proposals.

The "live performance" feel that drawing a sketch in front of someone conveys can be quite pleasing.

Also, your client can see the work in progress. While you are drawing, you or your client can point out any problems or mistakes that you might find. On the other hand, using a computer is an "operation" and it can be much harder to see the work in progress. This difference is the reason why I draw in the presence of my clients. Being particular about this (transparency/simplicity), I decided to write this book.

Initially, I intended to write down the time taken to draw each sketch (in seconds under the drawing) after closely monitoring things with a stopwatch. However, it turned out to just feel like a race against time. Moreover, being overly concerned with time can lead to one neglecting the most important thing: the drawing. In opposition to the idea of "faster is better", I realized that drawing at a moderate speed is fine and after that I was able to compile this book. As an example of what I am talking about, I would like to say that if the book says "3 min", I only meant that it would take somewhere around 3 min. That doesn't mean that you absolutely must done in 3 min. It doesn't matter if you take 5 minutes or more, I simply want you to try to learn to gauge just how quickly you are able to draw.

Mr. Hideo Shimizu, from Hideo Shimizu office Company Limited and Mr. Makoto Araie, from Araie Office, worked with me to create the manuscript for this book. Also, Mr. Satoru Ohta (formerly from Graphic-sha), editor of my previous publications, gave me much appreciated advice. Last but not least, to the editor of this book Mr. Hitoshi Mitomi, and to the designer, Mr. Hajime Kabutoya: I appreciate both of you being so kind as to adopt many of my unreasonable requests. It is because of your hard work that this wonderful book came to be. I also wish to express my gratitude to everyone else involved in the creation of this book.

Noriyoshi Hasegawa

1945	Born in Yokohama, Japan
1964	Graduated from Kanagawa Technical High School specializing in Industrial Design
	Nihon Gakki Seizo Kabushiki Gaisha (Currently Yamaha Co. Ltd.)
	In charge of designing musical instruments, furniture, logos, etc.
1987	Developed living space equipment
1988	In charge of designing architectural interior designs
1992	Yamaha Living Tech Co. Ltd., Chief Architectural Interior Designer
2005	Became Independent

[Current Primary Work]
Interior planning. Perspective drawing, designing logos.
Lectures on presentation techniques, etc.

[Publications]
Sketching Interiors: A Step-By-Step Guide
Sketching Interiors, Colour: A Step-By-Step Guide
Sketching Interiors: Coloured Pencils: A Step-By-Step Guide
Published from Graphic-sha Publishing Co., Ltd.

END

Interior Presentations
Techniques for Quick, Professional Renderings of Interiors

by Noriyoshi Hasegawa

Text and images copyright © 2016 Noriyoshi Hasegawa and Graphc-sha Publishing Co., Ltd.

First designed and published in Japan in 2016 by Graphic-sha Publishing Co., Ltd.

English edition published in 2018 by NIPPAN IPS Co., Ltd.

ISBN 9784865051445

First English Edition: April 2018

Printed in China

Original creative staff

Book design and layout:	Hajime Kabutoya (Happy and Happy)
Editor:	Hitoshi Mitomi (Graphic-sha Publishing Co., Ltd.)
Collaboration:	Hideo Shimizu office Company Limited, Araie Office, Satoru Ohta

English edition

English translation:	Kevin Wilson
English edition layout:	Shinichi Ishioka
Production and management:	Kumiko Sakamoto (Graphic-sha Publishing Co., Ltd.)

START!!
←